From one mother to another!
To Wendy - on your 50th
love, Mel. x

Barefoot *in* the Kitchen

Published by
The Bible Reading Fellowship
First Floor, Elsfield Hall
15–17 Elsfield Way, Oxford OX2 8FG

ISBN-10: 1 84101 346 3
ISBN-13: 978 1 84101 346 6
First published 2004
10 9 8 7 6 5 4 3 2 1
All rights reserved

Acknowledgments
Unless otherwise indicated, scripture quotations are taken from *The Living Bible*,
copyright © 1971 by Tyndale House Publishers

Scripture quotations taken from the Holy Bible, New International Version,
copyright © 1973, 1978, 1984 by International Bible Society, are used by
permission of Hodder & Stoughton Limited. All rights reserved. 'NIV' is a
registered trademark of International Bible Society. UK trademark number
1448790.

Scripture quotations marked (NLT) are taken from the Holy Bible, New Living
Translation, copyright © 1996. Used by permission of Tyndale House
Publishers, Inc., Wheaton, Illinois 60189. All rights reserved.

Scripture quotations taken from The New Revised Standard Version of the Bible,
Anglicized Edition, copyright © 1989, 1995 by the Division of Christian
Education of the National Council of the Churches of Christ in the USA, are
used by permission. All rights reserved.

A catalogue record for this book is available from the British Library

Printed in Singapore by Craft Print International Ltd

Barefoot *in* the Kitchen

BIBLE READINGS & REFLECTIONS
FOR MOTHERS

Alie Stibbe

Acknowledgments

Thanks are due primarily to God for getting me through the experiences that produced the material for this book, and to our four children who contributed in ways they will never begin to appreciate. Thanks also to Mark, my husband, who has shown unbelievable patience towards me over the years and enabled me to become who I am today.

Thanks to Naomi Starkey and all at BRF who have made this book possible: you are always a great encouragement to me.

Thanks to *Renewal* for granting permission for material from articles previously published there to be reworked for this book.

The devotional notes in this volume were published previously in *Day by Day with God*, BRF's Bible reading notes for women, and are used with permission. The notes have all been revised, in some cases rewritten and with additional material added.

Bible references that appear in the book unmarked are from the Living Bible. Other Bible translations used are the New Living Translation (NLT), the New International Version (NIV) and the New Revised Standard Version (NRSV) as marked.

Contents

Earth's crammed with heaven,
and every common bush afire with God;
but only she who sees
takes off her shoes...

AFTER

ELIZABETH BARRETT BROWNING

(1806–61)

Introduction

Therefore I am now going to allure her; I will lead her into the desert and speak tenderly to her. There I will give her back her vineyards, and will make the Valley of Achor [sorrow, tears, trouble] a door of hope.
HOSEA 2:14–15 (NIV)

Quite a few years ago now, when I was the mother of three children under the age of three years, I sat in church on one of the rare occasions I wasn't in the crèche and heard the preacher say that a person's spiritual life can often become a desert experience when they have young children. If he had found that as a father—and as someone paid to have a spiritual life—what must it be like for mothers, or other carers, who took the main brunt of the task without a break? I asked myself this question because I was totally lost in a spiritual wilderness—and I wasn't coping at all.

It took me a long time to begin to understand that the Lord had led me into that desert so that he could speak tenderly to me, woo me, give me back everything I felt I had lost, and more—so that he would eventually point me in the direction of an open door to a new reality, because he has promised us all a future and a hope. 'For I know the plans I have for you,' declares the Lord, 'plans to prosper you and not to harm you, plans to give you hope and a future' (Jeremiah 29:11, NIV).

I recently shared my testimony of the struggle I'd had as a young mother with a group consisting mainly of women, and realized that, although many things have changed for the better for young mothers, many still find themselves coping with the same problems and frustrations that I experienced, and can't see a way through. This encouraged me to gather up all the thoughts I had put down on paper during the time God was teaching me lessons of his love in my own personal wilderness, in the hope that what I'd learnt might be of benefit to those who now find themselves staring out on the same dry, rocky landscape.

You will find in this book a reworking of some of the monthly articles I wrote for *Renewal* during the two years when I was beginning to discover how to find the Lord in the ordinary things of domestic life. These articles have been interpersed with some of the early sets of Bible reading notes I wrote for *Day by Day with God*, a series of daily readings and meditations by women for women (and discerning men), published by BRF and Christina Press. A Bible passage is given for each of these readings, but only a small portion —a verse or two—is quoted in print, so it would be helpful to look up the reading in a Bible of your own (or on www.biblegateway.com).

I have introduced these articles and readings with an account of my own story. Although bits of this story have appeared in various articles over the years, I have never written it down as a whole before. I have always found it helpful to know that someone else has experienced what I am going through—that I am not alone in what I am feeling. Perhaps reading my testimony will help you put your own life into perspective and know that the Lord is beside you in your situation, however hopeless you might feel things are.

Finally, I have rounded the book off with some thoughts about what happens when we step through the door the Lord opens in our desert place and find ourselves in a new landscape, totally different from the wilderness we have left behind. Life inevitably goes in phases and moves on: small children grow up and our personal world begins to open out again. Knowing where the Lord is leading when we feel grass under our feet again, where there was once dry sand, can be a confusing experience—but one filled with promise and excitement.

Please use and enjoy this book at your own pace. It is a mixture of devotional aids and food for thought, all undated so that you can dip into it when it best fits into your schedule. I do hope and pray that the Lord speaks to you through what I have written and allures you in your desert place in the same way, if not in a greater way, that he allured me.

CAUTION

The operation of electrical kitchen appliances when not wearing shoes is potentially dangerous. Standing barefoot in the kitchen, as advocated in this book, is for purposes of prayerful meditation only. Please put your shoes back on before resuming domestic tasks.

Wandering in the Wilderness

How often they rebelled against him in the desert and grieved him in the wasteland!

PSALM 78:40 (NIV)

In this book I hope to share with those people, especially young mothers, who feel enclosed and trapped by their circumstances, a way in which we can find and experience God despite those restrictions. It is very difficult, when writing a book that intends to share some depth of spirituality, to approach the task without feeling totally unqualified to do it. You feel that people are bound to ask, 'Who is she, to think she has anything to say on this subject?' To try to answer this question, I thought it would be helpful to share some of my experiences, especially those surrounding my years of post-natal depression, including the moment that was to be God's linchpin in changing the direction of my whole life and the journey I took from there onwards.

In 1982 I was in my final year at university, determined to do post-graduate study with the hope of becoming a full-time academic. The last thing on my mind was marriage—and then, just when I wasn't looking, I met the man I knew I was destined to marry. The rest is history!

Although attitudes were changing, choices were quite different for women then than they are now. I obviously hadn't caught up with these changing attitudes, because it seemed unthinkable for me to move to a northern university to study for a doctorate if my future husband was going to be working in the south. Women today would probably choose to have their cake and eat it, and pursue a long-distance marriage relationship, but 20 years ago that wasn't on most women's agendas.

My plans to study were abandoned, and I was happy about that at the time. I also knew from the beginning that Mark intended studying for the ministry. After some thought and discussion, we decided that the most suitable thing for me to do as a prospective vicar's wife was to train as a teacher! How things have changed!

After being struck by a fifth-former during my last teaching practice, I wasn't keen to be a science teacher while Mark was training for the ministry. Instead, I ended up as a technician in the university research laboratory. Back in a scientific environment and talking to people in the know, I realized that I could easily have spent the three years of Mark's training doing the post-graduate research I had so wanted to do, as a *paid* research assistant, instead of doing the job I'd ended up with.

By this time, Mark's training was too far advanced for me to complete a scientific thesis in the time he had left at college. I don't think it would have mattered that much if I had enjoyed the job I was doing, but I hated it. I also didn't have the spiritual maturity to persevere in a difficult situation and ask God what he wanted to teach me through it. Instead, I allowed myself to become miserable, frustrated and full of self-pity.

In situations like this, we often need to fix the blame on another. Mark was enjoying his training, while I had a job I hated, so the focus of my bitterness became the church. If they'd only seen me as an individual during Mark's selection, and advised us as a couple, none of this would ever have happened—or so I thought.

Mark's first curacy was in the parish adjacent to the college. He was near enough to the university to finish his PhD part-time, and I managed to find a better job as a research assistant with the promise of registration for a doctorate attached. All seemed well.

Six months into my new job, there was still no mention of my research registration, so I went to see my project leader. He denied all knowledge of any such promise and said that he hoped I wasn't going to leave them in the lurch. Being a woman of principle, I adhered to my contract, but lost all enthusiasm. I did investigate an opportunity in another department, but it came to nothing. By this time, I was fuming under the surface, very unhappy and still unable to find God's direction. It seemed unfair that I had given up all my chances so that Mark could do the thing he wanted to do—or, more subtly, what God wanted him to do! I didn't realize that in failing to deal with my situation and attitude, I was storing up a lot of trouble for myself in the years to come.

My research contract finished a year before Mark was due to move. What could I do with that year? Thoughts turned to having a baby: I could have a baby before we moved to a university town, where I could start working towards my doctorate. But the best-laid plans come to nothing when the Lord is left out of the equation.

I had not anticipated post-natal depression. It was a terrible experience, especially as my male doctor seemed to think that a cup of black coffee and a good chat with the health visitor would cure me. I was an educated woman—so I had to pull myself together and get over it. I later discovered that I could have had proper treatment. Instead, I suffered in silence, despite feeling agoraphobic, suicidal and very much alone. The baby had colic; it cried incessantly and wouldn't sleep, which was physically and emotionally exhausting. As if that wasn't enough, I became pregnant again almost immediately. The lesson in that is never to test a new product for your health visitor!

The final year of Mark's curacy was thus a very taxing one. I tried to cope with two small babies; he moved his study out to another house in the parish so he could get some peace and quiet to finish writing up his thesis. The time to move didn't come a moment too soon.

I ought to have known that you can't run away from your problems; but a possible new start was all I could think of. Mark was now one of two curates in a large church in a northern university town. This was my chance: I applied to the university and started to look for a nanny, but another series of events overtook me. In the space of a week our car was vandalized, my mother died and I found I was pregnant again. Thinking of applying for a job was out of the question.

I resigned myself to my fate. I never considered that there might be light at the end of this tunnel, and I never talked about how I felt about my situation. The result was a continuing internal build-up of resentment and anger, which, every now and then, would burst forth. I remember throwing the contents of the draining rack out of the back door, in pure frustration.

The awful thing was that I knew exactly what I was like and what I was doing, but could do nothing about it. An added tension was that, all the time, I felt I had to keep up the façade of spirituality that befitted a curate's wife. Eventually I asked someone for help, but I was told I had to sort things out for myself. I never really understood that reaction from a woman in a church that was in the forefront of the 'inner healing' ministry. Maybe people still weren't ready to cope with the fact that leaders and their wives have problems just like other people. I know that things are largely different now.

I didn't read my Bible much during those first years after the three babies were born: I was too tired, too busy and too scared about what I might find there. When I did once open my Bible, a verse in Ephesians leapt out and convicted me: 'Get rid of all bitterness, rage and anger…' (Ephesians 4:31a, NIV).

I was bitter, I was angry, and I was prone to rage. I knew I had to do something about it—but what? If only I'd read the next verse, I might have found out 18 months sooner than I did: 'Be kind and compassionate to one another, forgiving each other, just as in Christ God forgave you' (v. 32, NIV).

The situation continued until my youngest was a year old. I thought I was doing OK; I was surviving despite the awful truth of how life really was, but I obviously wasn't doing as good a job as I thought at covering up the real me. The garbage in my life oozed out here and there, and left a nasty trail in its wake that I was too self-absorbed to notice. Others had noticed, and apparently those others had had enough. Two of the women in leadership in the church came to see me—and they wanted Mark to be present.

In my naïveté, I thought I was to be offered a leadership role in the children's work. I really needed to be needed, and I assumed that I was about to be included in ministry. How wrong I was!

Instead of being asked to come onboard and help, I was sat down and told that my attitude and behaviour had become totally unacceptable, that they were affecting members of the local community to which the group was trying to reach out, and that something had to be done—about me!

I really couldn't believe what I was hearing: it was not that I denied having a problem, but what surprised and hurt me was that one of the delegation was the woman I had asked to help me when we had first arrived. If my cry for help had been heard then, none of this would now have been necessary. I'm afraid I didn't stay to hear all they had to say: I locked myself in the bathroom and left Mark to see them to the door. I don't know how long I stayed in there, but I cried myself out.

What does one do in such a situation? Run away, become even more bitter, or what? I obviously couldn't change myself, so I was at a complete dead end. I'm not quite sure how it happened, because I don't remember praying or asking God for anything, but somehow he used this painful situation to prise open a chink in the door of my heart; then he stuck a big foot in it to prevent me slamming it shut again. I realized that it was now or never: I had to do something; it was like my last chance.

I came out of the bathroom and told Mark I wanted to have counselling. I knew I had to get myself sorted out, that I'd been wrong and I was sorry.

Two women counsellors from church came and listened to my story. One of them commented that she was surprised I was still in one piece after the things I had experienced (and I haven't told you the half). At last I felt that someone could see why I was the way I was—not that it was an excuse for what I was, but I was tired of people looking at the symptoms rather than the cause.

After more listening, I was prayed for very gently. I was encouraged to forgive all the people I felt had done me real or imaginary hurts throughout my life. It took a long time. Eventually, I came to the last thing and I couldn't make a sound. I struggled for words, but they would not come out. The only way I can describe it is to say it was like labour contractions in the chest, not the stomach. I struggled to control my breathing and eventually gasped out, 'I forgive.'

The most amazing inner change occurred instantly. I have never experienced anything like it before or since. I was aware that a huge burden had been lifted. I realized that forgiveness has its own dynamic and that until I had forgiven others, I couldn't see the things that I needed God to forgive me for. I was suddenly hit by my part in all the hurts that I felt others had inflicted on me. I had to spend a long time asking God to forgive me for words and actions in which I had never imagined I had been at fault.

Although I was now free, the whole process left me feeling incredibly raw—a horrible but wonderful rawness that lasted for several weeks. That evening was the turning point that will always stand out in my mind, the beginning of a spiritual journey that led to the discoveries I share in this book. Things didn't fall into place at once; I had a lot of people to apologize to and it took time. I withdrew from church life for a year—a valuable time of convalescence in which God continued to heal my wounds.

During that year I had a faithful visitor. She turned up on my doorstep unannounced one morning and helped me with the children, and she left me with a valuable lesson I shall never forget. I asked her why she visited me when no one else did, and why she persisted in helping me with the babies. She told me that she had learned from her experience with someone else that external appearances often betray what lies underneath. She knew I'd been the way I was for a reason, and that acceptance and patient love were what was needed to see my sort of person through. I have never forgotten that, and it has made me more understanding of difficult people I have met over the years. Don't you ever forget it either!

My inner healing and year of convalescence was God's wonderful timing to prepare me to take on the role of a vicar's wife. Without it, Mark would probably have left the ministry and returned to academic life. A parish is hard enough to cope with, without having to cope with the sort of person I had been.

'The wise woman builds her house, but with her own hands the foolish one tears hers down' (Proverbs 14:1, NIV).

This time I was prepared for God's new start—not the one I might have planned, but one that he knew was best for me. Not that everything was suddenly a bed of roses: almost a year after our move, I miscarried a few weeks into a pregnancy, which was a traumatic event that took a while to come to terms with.

In the summer I had written to the editor of *Renewal* in response to an article in their women's column, and the editor asked me to be a regular contributor. Now, in the autumn, I began to write about my spiritual journey. I wrote for the magazine for two years. Each month I took my life apart in front of the readers, and the Lord taught me one lesson after another about finding him in the situation in which he had placed me.

This book retraces my spiritual journey out of the wilderness, and I'd like you to come with me, especially if you are one of the ten per cent of women who suffer from post-natal depression, and particularly if you fall into the category, like me, of the one in four of those women whose post-natal depression is never diagnosed and treated.

Trust in the Lord with all your heart and lean not on your own understanding; in all your ways acknowledge him, and he will make your paths straight.
PROVERBS 3:5–6

Some of the material in this chapter has been reworked from 'Be Honest about Your Feelings' and 'The Key to Inner Healing', which were printed in *Renewal* in May 1994 and April 1994 respectively.

Living in his presence

Then Moses said to [the Lord], 'If your Presence does not go with us, do not send us up from here… What else will distinguish me and your people from all the other people on the face of the earth?'
EXODUS 33:15–16 (NIV)

Moses is about to lead the people of Israel through the wilderness to the promised land. The Lord tells Moses that he will now only send an angel to guide them, because they worshipped a golden calf. Moses pleads with God for his own presence rather than an angel, because if the people of God are not living in the Lord's presence, what will make them any different from anyone else?

After my radical experience of healing from post-natal depression, I knew I was about to set out on a journey of rediscovering my relationship with the Lord. I had no idea where this journey would lead, but I did know that I needed God's presence. Only the Lord's presence would lift my ordinary daily life into the extraordinary, make mundane tasks any different from any other task, and make any difference in me.

The following readings reflect aspects of how I learnt to recognize God's presence. As you read them, remember God's words to Moses: 'My Presence will go with you and I will give you rest' (Exodus 33:14, NIV). What a great promise: make it yours!

Longing for God

PSALM 38:9 (NIV)

All my longings lie open before you, O Lord; my sighing is not hidden from you.

I was at a prayer meeting that was full of young mothers, some with babies and toddlers present. As we were led in worship, the children were playing noisily behind the sofa and running in and out of the kitchen. One of the mothers, whose children were at infant school, was completely lost in the worship. 'If only I had half a chance,' I thought, as I stood up to retrieve baby Sam, who'd shuffled out of sight. As I sat down again, the mother next to me had also come back from supervising a toddler. She burst into tears. 'Are you all right?' I asked, knowing she couldn't possibly be!

'No,' she said, 'I just want to be in God's presence, but I have to keep going to sort out my child!'

'I know what you mean,' I replied. It was not the place for a lengthy talk, but I prayed in my heart that it might help her to know that the vicar's wife was in the same situation and just as frustrated as she was.

This woman has been on my heart and mind ever since. What could be done? When I was first asked to write Bible reading notes, I felt I wanted to try to help people like her, like me—and like you? So many mothers long to be able to come freely into God's presence in worship, to be able to raise hands free of babies and children, to listen to the sermon 'live' and to have the opportunity to be ministered to in prayer or have time alone to read God's word and pray. When I came across Psalm 38:9, it was like a sigh of relief in itself, being reminded that the Lord knows all my sighs and longings already and—more than that—it is OK to sigh. The Lord has great compassion and not criticism for mothers and their children.

If you have a minute to collapse in a comfy chair, lie back, close your eyes and tell the Lord the simple longings of your heart. Perhaps write them down. Let his Holy Spirit minister his compassion and understanding to you.

*

Meeting with God

PSALM 42:1–2 (NIV)

As the deer pants for streams of water, so my soul pants for you, O God. My soul thirsts for God, for the living God. When can I go and meet with God?

Before I was married and had children, there was a time when I could come before the Lord like the deer coming down to the watering hole in the early morning, before the day became too hot, and in the cool of the evening before the night's rest. I didn't believe the person who preached at the student Christian Union and said, 'Spend time with the Lord now in prayer and reading his word, because you will never have so much time again.' How true that statement turned out to be! Now I am often like the hunted deer in this reading from Psalm 42, running with no time or place to stop.

Finding time to stop and draw apart with God has become more and more difficult with the birth of each of our four children and the development of my husband's ministry. I am sure many Christian mums often feel the same—very thirsty, very dry and crying out like the psalmist, 'Where can I find him to come and stand before him?' and 'When can I find him?' Even the bathroom and the loo provide little privacy with babies and toddlers about!

I spent my first years as a mother under enormous guilt because I had no daily quiet time. Then gradually I realized that if I wanted to be in the Lord's presence enough, I had to find new and imaginative ways of meeting with him, rather as two young lovers forbidden to meet can come up with innovative plans to do just that. I also had to allow the Lord Jesus to free me from the condemnation that I had heaped upon myself for not being able to come regularly to the watering hole, and ask him to start to show me other ways I could quench my spiritual thirst.

Thank you, Lord, that you know everything about me. Free me from my burden of self-condemnation so that I can see the paths that you have prepared for me to walk in and the places I can be with you. Amen

*

God is with us

PSALM 139:7–8 (NIV)

Where can I go from your Spirit? Where can I flee from your presence? If I go up to the heavens, you are there; if I make my bed in the depths, you are there.

Psalm 139 has always been precious to me. When I begin to feel like the hunted deer, these verses help me to remember that I don't actually have to draw aside to be in the presence of the Lord, but that I am always in his presence whatever I'm doing. When we have those 'heavenly' moments in our walk with God, it is easy to know that he is with us. For mothers, however, there are many moments when we are in 'the depths' and God seems very far away. This is particularly so for those who, through no fault of their own, have suffered from post-natal depression. Even in that situation we are in God's presence, although we do not feel it.

It can be hard to know God's presence on a day-to-day basis even when we are well and coping. We need to learn to recognize his presence, so that wherever we are and whatever we are doing, we can communicate with him without having to draw aside physically. All it needs is practice, but that is easier said than done!

One well-known teacher of this doctrine was the 17th-century monk, Brother Lawrence, who spent many years working in a kitchen. Despite the fact that he didn't have four children pulling at his habit strings and the phone ringing constantly, I am sure we can learn something from him.

It is only necessary to realize that God is intimately present within us, to turn every moment to him and ask for his help, recognize his will in all things doubtful and to do well all that he requires of us, offering what we do to him before we do it, and giving thanks for having done it afterwards. In this unbroken communion one is continually preoccupied with praising, worshipping and loving God for his infinite acts of loving kindness and perfection.[1]

✳

Holy ground

PSALM 27:4

The one thing I want from God, the thing I seek most of all, is the privilege of meditating in his Temple, living in his presence every day of my life, delighting in his incomparable perfections and glory.

In the previous reading, I introduced you to Brother Lawrence. Unlike the psalmist, he did not have the privilege of being able to gaze upon the beauty of the Lord and seek him in his temple, as he served in the monastery kitchen. By constantly turning his inward gaze upon Jesus, however, the kitchen became just like the temple for him.

One thing that Brother Lawrence and those who served in the temple did have in common was that they both went about barefoot. For the temple priest, taking off his shoes was an act of reverence, indicating he was on holy ground. Monks are taught that even the ordinary things of life should be treated as sacred, so Lawrence, washing up wooden bowls barefoot in his kitchen, would probably have considered his task comparable with serving God in the temple, cleansing sacred vessels.

In my mind, this leads to the conclusion that a kitchen floor could be considered 'holy ground' if we are dedicated to seeking God in our kitchens through the tasks we perform there. Paul encourages us to do everything in the name of the Lord Jesus, giving thanks to God the Father through him (Colossians 3:17), and I believe that applies as much to stacking the dishwasher and taking out the rubbish as it does to leading a Bible study or helping in church. If we considered our kitchens or places of work holy ground upon which we could serve the Lord, wouldn't that make our yokes easy and our burdens light?

Go into your kitchen or place of work and take off your shoes.
As you stand barefoot on the floor, ask God to bless and
consecrate that place so that you can serve him there
in his presence from now on.

Barefoot meditation

PSALM 15:1–2 (NIV)

Lord, who may dwell in your sanctuary? Who may live on your holy hill? He whose walk is blameless and who does what is righteous, who speaks the truth from his heart.

When you stand on a kitchen floor barefoot even for a short time, you realize how cold it is: it gets you in touch with reality. When you take off your shoes, you also notice that you are not as tall as you'd like to think! That is exactly what happens when we come into the Lord's presence: we become aware of the reality of our sinfulness. We are humbled and cut down to our actual size. There we can stand and realize that nothing we think we are now, nor anything we have done in the past, counts to our credit in the Lord's sight. Yet we must not forget that we are infinitely precious to him.

This happened to Isaiah when he saw the Lord in the temple. His immediate reaction was to cry, 'Woe to me! I am ruined! For I am a man of unclean lips, and I live among a people of unclean lips, and my eyes have seen the King, the Lord Almighty' (Isaiah 6:5, NIV). Isaiah knew that whatever came out of his mouth was unclean and came from an unclean heart. An unclean heart breeds evil thoughts, words and actions. Jesus himself said, 'The evil man brings evil things out of the evil stored up in his heart' (Luke 6:45, NIV).

Psalm 15:1–2 indicates that those who want to dwell in God's sanctuary, to live on his holy hill and constantly enter his presence, must *be* blameless, *do* what is righteous, and *speak* truth from the heart. Only the redeeming work of the Lord Jesus Christ can effect that change in our hearts and lives. If we want to live in God's presence, we must ask Jesus Christ to cleanse our hearts and change our lives.

Since we have confidence to enter the Most Holy Place by the blood of Jesus… let us draw near to God with a sincere heart in full assurance of faith, having our hearts sprinkled to cleanse us from a guilty conscience (Hebrews 10:19, 22, NIV).

*

A clean heart

PSALM 51:10–11 (NIV)

Create in me a pure heart, O God, and renew a steadfast spirit within me. Do not cast me from your presence or take your Holy Spirit from me.

These verses are taken from the prayer King David prayed after he had committed adultery with Bathsheba. He was acutely aware that what he had done would mean exclusion from God's presence and the removal of the indwelling of God's Holy Spirit. I feel constantly aware that the sins in my life keep me from the Lord's presence and grieve his Spirit. There is no avoiding the issue, pretending they are not there or didn't happen. Often I say to my children when they need disciplining, 'Just tell me what happened. All I want is the truth; then I won't need to get cross. Tell it as it is and we will sort it out.'

The Lord deals with me just like those naughty children, and, just like them, I start making excuses and playing the problem down, when an honest confession is all that it takes. After a while, the little sins pile up and become a big weight. It is usually after yelling at the children about nothing that I cry out to God, over a sink full of washing-up, 'I am sorry! My heart is full of junk and I've blown it again. Create in me a clean heart and renew a right spirit within me.'

Once you have tasted how good it is to live in God's presence, you will definitely want to try to keep a clean sheet with the Lord, rather than trying to live without him. We should confess as we go through the day—stop and put the wrong thing right so that we don't allow it to mess up our next experience. I know a tune that fits today's verses and I often sing it to keep my heart in an attitude of repentance and to focus my mind on the Lord.

Make a card with these words from Psalm 51 written on it. Put it over the sink, by the kettle or on your desk. Memorize the verses and use them as a prayer throughout the day. Maybe you know a tune that fits them too. Let your plea come to God, by singing or recollection; let it bring you constantly into his presence and the knowledge of his Holy Spirit.

*

Count your blessings

PSALM 103:1–2 (NIV)

Praise the Lord, O my soul; all my inmost being, praise his holy name. Praise the Lord, O my soul, and forget not all his benefits.

Praising the Lord with all that is within us is an excellent way to keep ourselves in his presence and aware of him all day long. When we dwell on the fact that we have been forgiven and cleansed of our sin by God because of Christ's death for us, our whole inmost being wells up to bursting point with gratitude. For me, when my soul, the innermost depths of me, is almost leaping in silent praise despite the task I am doing, then I feel that I am living in awareness of the Lord's presence to the best of my ability in my situation. Unfortunately for me, those moments of rapture are usually when I am alone and occupied in a quiet, monotonous task requiring little thought… like peeling vegetables. There are not many times like that in our house, and the trick is to carry on the inner attitude of praise even when distracted. How?

The first thing I have to make myself do when interrupted is to bless the distracting person in the attitude of my heart, and not begrudge them my attention because they have torn me from full focus on the Lord. If you begrudge them, you lose all the 'holy ground' you thought you'd gained. If your heart has an attitude of blessing and compassion when interrupted, though, it allows you to carry that inner praise and blessing into the interruption and to thank God for his 'outward' benefits. The little child pulling at your skirt is a blessing, as is ministering to his needs. It is good to cultivate the 'gratitude attitude', to count our blessings and praise God for them inwardly in our hearts and outwardly by our actions.

Got to go—someone's interrupting, bless him!

Ask the Lord for a heart and mind that is consciously going to praise him in all things today. Acknowledge and count your blessings as you go along.

A singing day

PSALM 100:1–2 (NIV)

Shout for joy to the Lord, all the earth. Worship the Lord with gladness; come before him [i.e. into his presence] with joyful songs.

Quiet, overwhelming, inward praise is one thing, but you just have to let it out sometimes! I like to sing when I am working in the kitchen or the laundry. When we sing to the Lord, we become aware of his presence.

Singing can encompass many moods. I have already touched on singing as a means of maintaining an attitude of repentance. Music somehow enables us to express a depth of emotion that words alone just cannot do. I like to sing cheerful songs of praise and quieter songs of worship to keep me aware of the Lord. I really do hope no one is listening when I start on the old choruses I learned as a child! The teaching they contain has become a foundation for my faith, and when I need reminding about some biblical truth, I can usually find an old chorus to help and encourage me to hang in there.

Maybe you haven't got such a repertoire. If you are stuck, a good way to sing to the Lord is by using a cassette or CD of worship songs to guide you. The songs you sing don't have to be sophisticated: often the simpler they are, the better. Eventually, before you know it, the song is internalized and will pop into your head unprompted at odd moments of the day. When that happens, you know that your life is becoming undergirded with a river of praise to the Lord that can burst out in your mind or through your mouth, rather than the less desirable lyrics of some secular songs. This is what Paul means when he talks about singing sacred songs and making melody in your hearts to the Lord (Ephesians 5:19).

Today is a singing day. Don't worry about feeling foolish! If you don't want to sing alone, sort out your CDs and find something to inspire you as you work, or decide to go to your nearest Christian bookshop and look for something new.

*

Feeding on the word

PSALM 119:97 (NIV)

Oh, how I love your law! I meditate on it all day long.

Reading God's word makes us more aware of his presence and provides a means by which we can hear his voice. At a young mums' Bible study, we were almost competing to see who had left it the longest since opening their Bible! No doubt we all loved God's word, but having a young family means not being able to dig deep into a Bible passage and gnaw over it like our dog does with a bone, having a jolly good chew for an hour or so. It is easy to think that if we can't have a feast, then we have to have a total fast. Not so; we just have to find other ways of feeding on the word.

If you have a repetitive task to do, listening to a tape of a Bible exposition or watching a teaching video may be the answer. Even this can be difficult without losing track of what is being said, so I try to 'snack on the word', or, as the psalmist puts it, 'meditate on it all day long'. A snack is better than no food at all, and eating little and often can be good for you.

How can you snack on the word? You need a means of providing a verse a day at a glance—sort of biblical 'fast food'—such as an old-fashioned scripture calendar. Place it where you can see it first thing in the morning and then throughout the day (next to the kettle is a good place). Read the verse and let it sink in. Then let your subconscious chew on it all day. Perhaps base your praying and praising around It. Ask God to give you insight into the verse and to speak to you through it. Read it again as you make your bedtime drink and review your meditations as you drift off to sleep.

In this way we can allow the word of God to dwell in us richly and the Holy Spirit can prompt us with the 'snacks' we've ingested, just at our moment of need.

Lord, free me from my guilt concerning Bible study. Help me to find realistic ways of feeding on your word in my situation.

*

Through the night

PSALM 63:6 (NIV)

On my bed I remember you; I think of you through the watches of the night.

Before I was a mother, I thought how noble it must be to spend a whole night awake in prayer. How did people do it? Four children later, and I am dying for a night of unbroken sleep! My fourth baby keeps me just conscious, if not totally awake, most of the night. It can get very boring just staring at the ceiling as I lie in bed with him, so I try to spend those waking moments in silent conversation with the Lord, which is rather more constructive than counting sheep.

I tell him about the day past, running through it in thanks and confession and trying to see how I could have handled things better. I pray about the day ahead and cast all my anxieties on him, from trying to find time to do the mending to understanding the new-format tax form. It gives me a wonderful sense of peace, and if I fall asleep I carry on praying when I wake up again. I also use the time for serious intercession, praying for the needs of people I know and their various situations. I pray for our church and the people in it. I also pray for members of my family and other people I know who don't yet trust Jesus as Saviour. I trust the Holy Spirit to put the right person into my mind as I go along.

Often I think back over what God has done for me and my family. Sometimes it is good just to be quiet and rest in God's arms, just as the baby is resting in mine, and allow the Holy Spirit, the Comforter, to minister to my inward needs. It is quite amazing how quickly a wakeful night passes when you spend it with the Lord. Before you know it, it's time to get up and somehow you don't feel quite as tired as you would have done if you'd watched the clock all night long.

Lord, help me to spend my wakeful moments in the night talking with you. I ask that I might meet with you in a special way at those times. Amen

*

Making space

PSALM 5:1–3

O Lord, hear me praying; listen to my plea, O God my king, for I will never pray to anyone but you. Each morning I will look to you in heaven and lay my requests before you praying earnestly.

Even when we are consciously trying to live in continual awareness of God's presence with us, there is still room for a specific prayer time when we can draw aside and pray earnestly to the Lord. I try hard to think of a better time than the morning. The morning is a new beginning and a natural time to reacquaint ourselves with the Lord by setting time aside to be alone with him, but I know how terribly difficult this is. Often my morning prayer is only a minute or two as I sit on the edge of the bed, or a quick plea for strength and patience as I hide in the loo.

I treasure the 15 minutes my husband and I have praying together when I get back from taking the children to school. We pray for the day ahead, for each other and the children and the people we are committed to praying for regularly. I still wish I had more time alone, however, and I have to recognize and grab those times when they come—for example, walking up to school or pottering in the garden when the baby is asleep in his pushchair. What is important is making time for God.

I have recently realized that there is no excuse not to try, even if we are well out of practice! Your simple prayer does matter in the light of eternity, so don't be fooled into thinking you can't make a difference. When I was a young Christian I was taught the rhyme, 'Satan trembles when he sees the weakest Christian on her knees.' And that means you!

Take an honest, critical look at your schedule for the last week. Was there a time when you could have given something up and found ten minutes a day to spend in concentrated prayer? Ask the Lord to help you grab those spaces from now on.

*

When we fail

PSALM 101:2

I will try to walk a blameless path, but how I need your help, especially in my own home, where I long to act as I should.

I should have pinned this verse above the sink this week. My husband has been away and I have been caring for the children and trying to write my Bible reading notes in whatever space I could find. Every morning I have prayed that I might be able to walk a blameless path, especially at home with the children. But don't they always know which buttons to press to get you irritated, especially when you feel vulnerable and under pressure? Mine certainly do! Every day I have failed and felt quite bereft of God's help when I needed it most. But of course he was right there, standing next to me laughing, saying, 'Woman, stop exasperating these children of yours! Be quiet and give them the big hug that they need, not all this condemnation!'

Like Paul, 'I do not understand what I do. For what I want to do I do not do, but what I hate to do… For I have the desire to do what is good, but I cannot carry it out' (Romans 7:15, 18b, NIV). Thankfully, we can be rescued from this dilemma through Jesus Christ our Lord, who frees us from the bondage of our sinful nature. The spiritual discipline of practising God's presence should be keeping us in a place where God's love can touch and change us.

Even when we fail, we have a wonderful Saviour who can, by his cleansing and forgiveness, bring us back into that close fellowship with the Father.

O Lord, you know that my inner desire is to live continually in your presence. You know the turmoil I experience when I do not allow your Holy Spirit to rule in my heart, mind and actions. Lord, today give me the humility to stop when I am out of line, to ask you to forgive me and put me back on track, especially in my own home. I ask this for the praise of your glorious name. Amen.

*

No moaning

PSALM 19:14 (NIV)

May the words of my mouth and the meditation of my heart be pleasing in your sight, O Lord, my Rock and my Redeemer.

Often by necessity rather than by nature, we mothers often have to make an active choice to be like Martha rather than like Mary—to be cooking for hordes rather than sitting on the front row of this week's Bible conference. There are two important things to note here: first, that the family should not be used as an excuse not to seek the Lord's presence; and second, that if we have been given a family to care for, we should not complain about those who have the freedom to 'sit at Jesus' feet' either in private or public worship.

It occurred to me the other day that Jesus was not criticizing Martha for preparing dinner, but for fretting and complaining about it.

Wouldn't you rather be Mary rather than Martha, getting it all first-hand rather than overheard and second-hand, diluted by the distractions of domestic life?

The Lord knows that your inner desire is to be sitting at his feet. He knows where you are and your responsibilities and ties. If you look in John 11, you will see that Martha is as dear to Jesus as her sister is. He has much compassion in his heart for her, and thus, I am sure, for us. It is important that we grasp and accept what we cannot change about our lives, not spoiling the beautiful thing that the Lord is trying to grow in our hearts, by complaining, self-pity and attention seeking. These negative attitudes are not compatible with a woman who is seeking to walk in God's presence, even in a kitchen. Psalm 39:1 says 'I am going to quit complaining! I'll keep quiet, especially when the ungodly are around me.' I know I could do with taking that advice. A moaning Christian is not a good advert for the kingdom of God.

Make Psalm 19:14 your prayer for the day. Is there anything you need to stop moaning about and accept? Bring it before the Lord.

*

In God's presence

PSALM 84:3

Even the sparrows and swallows are welcome to come and nest among your altars and there have their young, O Lord of heaven's armies, my King and my God!

I have chosen the verse above because it shows us that even the commonest small drab bird is welcome to make itself at home in the place that symbolizes the presence of an all-powerful God. Sometimes, if you are at home all day, it can be very easy to begin to feel you are worthless because you cannot make a significant contribution outside the home, especially at church. Despite how the secular world may view 'stay-at-home' women, they too are infinitely precious. Jesus says in Luke 12:6 that not one sparrow, valued at five for a penny, is forgotten by God, and he encourages us not to fear, because we are worth more than many sparrows to him.

I am sure God must feel as much overwhelming pride and joy watching us make those first tentative, lurching steps towards walking in his presence as a mother does, watching her little ones taking their first few steps. My smallest started walking this week, and keeps landing with a bump, but he gets up to try again and claps with pleasure. So I think we should give ourselves a clap when we make some progress in practising God's presence, even if we do land with a bump now and again. If we resolve to keep on trying until discipline becomes habit (and the 'experts' say it only takes six weeks of persistence to change or form a new habit), we will find ourselves and, as a result, our children, nesting right in the crevices of the altar of the Lord's presence.

Thank you, Lord, for loving us with an infinitely special love, and that we can walk in your presence in the ordinariness of our everyday lives. Help us, by the power and freedom given by your Holy Spirit, to practise your presence so that the conscious act becomes an intuitive habit. We ask this so that others might see you in us and desire to know you as a constant, life-changing presence in their own hearts. Amen

---

1   Brother Lawrence, *The Practice of the Presence of God*, trans. E.K. Blaiklock (Hodder & Stoughton, 1981), pp. 28–29

Barefoot in the kitchen

Then Joshua fell face down to the ground in reverence, and asked him, 'What message does my Lord have for his servant?' The commander of the Lord's army replied, 'Take off your sandals, for the place where you are standing is holy.' And Joshua did so.
JOSHUA 5:14b–15 (NIV)

'Pregnant, barefoot and in the kitchen!' Many of us have heard this well-worn phrase that was intended to keep a woman firmly in her 'allotted place', but it doesn't go down very well these days: women are more likely to want to be slim, well-shod and in the boardroom. Nevertheless, however successful we were before we had children, many of us find ourselves in exactly that domestic situation.

If the domestic situation is not one you want to be or enjoy being in, the feeling of being trapped can be overwhelming. The resentment begins to grow, and the chances of constructive personal use of that time decrease progressively. The early years of motherhood become something not to be enjoyed but to be endured until we have the opportunity to return to the place where we feel we might find some self-fulfilment.

For some women, returning to work after having a child is a necessity and not an option; yet, however enlightened contemporary society claims to be, many women find that they are stuck at home for several years until all the children are at school. Ten years can be a large chunk of life to while away, wishing you were somewhere else—and is easily wasted if not used constructively.

By the time I came to that realization, three years had gone by. I know that no time or experience is wasted in God's economy, but think what he could have achieved in my life if I'd allowed things to be different! It's no use crying over the past, though. It's better to lay a course for the future. I began to investigate how life could be lived fruitfully in an enclosed environment—because that's how I found mothering young babies—enclosed and isolating. With this thought in mind, I considered how people endured a commitment to live a cloistered religious life. The only thing I had in common with such people was a basic commitment to my 'enclosed' lifestyle —one that, like them, I had chosen out of conscious obedience. What I wanted to do was to find out how the way they enacted their commitment could help me in my situation, stuck at home in my own domestic cloister.

Very soon I came across the Rule of St Benedict. Benedict was the founder of an order of monks who were committed to lifelong enclosure within a monastic community. With the wrong attitude, such a commitment would be a harsh sentence, but the promises the monks made helped them to work out their commitment on a daily basis. One of their promises is the practice of *stability*—a spiritual attitude that, practised in the confines of the community, can help a person find a path to God.

What is 'stability' and what can it mean for those in an enclosed domestic situation? For mothers with post-natal depression, 'stable' is the last thing they feel! We are not necessarily looking for emotional stability: that will come in due time when working out your commitment. What is meant by 'stability' is an ongoing, willing acceptance of the enclosed situation in which we find ourselves, and a commitment to a loving relationship with the people in community with us, however difficult they are.

For the mother at home, struggling with the restrictions of young children, stability means an ongoing acknowledgment in the following vein:

Yes, God, you have placed me in this situation with these children for however long it is you have planned. I accept the situation I am in. I accept these children you have blessed me with, and I ask that you will help me to be committed to a daily loving relationship with this family for as long as it takes.

To allow God's stability into our hearts, to agree with and accept what he has willed for us at this present moment, is to relinquish the inner struggle that constantly nags and says, 'There must be more to life than this!' It allows God to work creatively in our situation with surprising results. It is the attitude that allowed Mary to say to the angel Gabriel, 'I am the Lord's servant. May it be to me as you have said' (Luke 1:38, NIV). This is not an easy statement for a woman to make in the climate of current secular attitudes, but it is essential for not only the spiritual but also the emotional and physical welfare of the person who has made a commitment to 'enclosure'.

You may feel that I'm suggesting the impossible, but note that the angel says to Mary, 'Nothing is impossible with God' (Luke 1:37, NIV). These aren't changes that we make in our own strength, but in co-operation with God's Holy Spirit working inside us. This is the essence of what Richard Foster means when he says, 'Spiritual disciplines allow us to place ourselves before God so that he can transform us.'[1] The ongoing act of accepting our situation is the discipline that puts us in the place where God can make us the person he planned us to be. That place—in this case, the home— is 'holy ground', and we should treat it as such.

For mums, saying 'yes' to their situation is saying 'yes' to the kitchen. A great deal of our time is spent there. In accepting our situation, the kitchen becomes our temple, a place in which we can encounter the presence of God and learn to worship him on a very unlikely sort of 'holy ground'.

If we are willing to accept our situation as holy ground where God can reach and change us, what then? When Moses (Exodus 3:5) and Joshua (Joshua 5:15) encountered the presence of the living God, they were told to take off their shoes, because the place on which they were standing was holy ground. Taking off shoes was an act of reverence and submission—reverence for God and submission to what he was about to ask of them.

How can we apply this in our domestic situation? I don't think it's terribly practical to promise always to go barefoot in the kitchen: I once had a kitchen floor that was so cold I used to get cramp in my feet after a minute without slippers on. However, it is interesting to note that Brother Lawrence, the monk who practised the presence of God in the kitchen where he worked, was a member of a barefoot monastic order.[2]

Nevertheless, it might be a good practical exercise to find a quiet moment alone to go into your kitchen, take off your shoes and spend some time allowing God to 'take you captive' (or maybe 'captivate you', if that is a more helpful image). In biblical times, captives were always held barefoot, not only to stop them running away, but to signify their submission (2 Chronicles 28:15; Isaiah 20:2–4). Now is the time to tell God that you are not going to run away any longer from the situation you hate—that you are going to submit to it because it can be a holy place where you know you can meet him if you are open to his voice.

When you take off your shoes as an act of commitment, three things happen:

• As I mentioned earlier, you are literally 'brought down to size', especially if you take off high heels.
• You get in touch with reality through the soles of your feet, especially if the floor is cold, damp or sticky.
• You will find your natural stance, as you will not have any shoe heels pulling your back out of shape.

Removing our shoes is a humbling act: it provides God with a chance to show us ourselves as we really are in the light of his presence. Although we are each special in God's sight, there is now room for us to acknowledge that, in relation to God himself we are nothing; we can face up to the truth about ourselves. As the psalmist says, 'Surely you desire truth in the inner parts; you teach me wisdom in the inmost place' (Psalm 51:6, NIV).

This can be very painful, but if we are willing to have this level of openness and vulnerability before God, we will find ourselves in a place of peace and contentment that we could never have imagined. Strange as it may seem, we will begin to understand what Christ meant when he said, 'Then you will know the truth, and the truth will set you free' (John 8:32, NIV).

I found that removing my shoes, being cut down to size and getting in touch with reality produced a sense of mourning in me over all the bad attitudes that had accumulated in my life, but God used this to reinforce what he was teaching me: in the Bible, people who mourned went about barefoot (2 Samuel 15:30). It seemed that part of the process of commitment and finding God on my patch of holy ground involved mourning over the past so that a genuine act of repentance could take place, so that I could know God's forgiveness and be prepared by his Spirit for what lay ahead. Jesus' words about mourners being comforted became very real (Matthew 5:4). When we are truly sorry for our past, the forgiveness we receive in the present is truly comforting. In humbling ourselves, we put ourselves in a position where God can meet us, even if it means that we have to shed some tears. 'Submit yourselves, then, to God... Come near to God and he will come near to you... Grieve, mourn... Humble yourselves before the Lord, and he will lift you up' (James 4:7–10, NIV).

When we remove our shoes, we also find our natural stance. Through our humility and acceptance, God can reveal to us the person he intended us to be. I must emphasize that I didn't find the 'real me' in a flash of revelation when I first took off my shoes; the process took a few years of 'shoe shedding', and led me through many stages of understanding as God revealed area after area of my life that needed sorting out. What is important at the initial point of submission and commitment is realizing that this is the beginning of an exciting journey, not an instant makeover.

In Romans 12:2, Paul shows us the ongoing process of becoming the person God intends us to be: 'Do not conform any longer to the pattern of this world, but be transformed by the renewing of your mind. Then you will be able to test and approve what God's will is—his good, pleasing and perfect will' (NIV). Although the English verb 'be transformed' implies a once-off happening, the Greek verb is continuous.

The take-home message of all this is *not* that mothers must accept old-fashioned perceptions of submissiveness propagated by a male-dominated society: please don't assume that. What I am saying is that if we stop struggling against what God has for us in the different phases of our life, then we can experience blessing, growth and deeper spiritual understanding in the present, which will prepare us for what the Lord has in store for us in the future. Our *now* is a gift—that's why it's called 'the present', you see! Are you ready to unwrap it?

---

1   R.A. Foster, *Celebration of Discipline* (Hodder & Stoughton, 1989), p. 7.
2   Brother Lawrence, *The Practice of the Presence of God*, translated by E.M. Blaiklock (Hodder & Stoughton, 1981), p. 13.

Take off your shoes

All of you, clothe yourselves with humility toward one another, because, 'God opposes the proud but gives grace to the humble.' Humble yourselves, therefore, under God's mighty hand, that he may lift you up in due time.

1 PETER 5:5–6 (NIV)

The following Bible readings will give you a chance to examine more closely some of the ideas I mentioned in the preceding chapter. These readings follow on from the ones about living in God's presence and they touch on many lessons that the Lord taught me during my children's pre-school years—especially lessons about the nature of humility and servanthood.

The verses above have always been of great encouragement to me because they helped me to understand that the difficult, humbling tasks of motherhood were only for a time and that the Lord would eventually lift me out of them. Children grow up quickly and we only spend a very short time on our knees at their level. Now I am very grateful to God for the lessons he taught me in those years; even though they were very challenging, they stood me in good stead for the future. I hope that the following readings help you to take advantage of the unique opportunity offered by being the mother of small children.

Barefoot in God's presence

EXODUS 3:1–12 (NIV)

'Do not come any closer,' God said. 'Take off your sandals, for the place where you are standing is holy ground.'

On my kitchen windowsill I have a rather unusual icon. An icon is a religious picture that is kept in a prominent place so as to catch the eye and draw the thoughts back to God. My icon is of Moses on Mount Sinai, removing his shoes in front of the burning bush in the presence of the Lord. Many people who see it ask what it is doing there. You may wonder too!

The icon reminds me that God told Moses to take off his shoes, because, being in the Lord's presence, the ground where he was standing was holy. I like to think of my kitchen as holy ground, as I try to seek the Lord's presence during all the time I spend there serving others for him. I am also reminded that Moses was a humble man (Numbers 12:3) and that the removal of his shoes was an indication of his willingness to be obedient to God's intentions for his life. For me, bare feet have become a symbol of my acceptance of God's role for me at the present time and an acknowledgment that, in God's sight, my kitchen is holy ground because he knows that I have chosen to serve him there.

In the Bible, four groups of people regularly went barefoot. One group were the priests in the temple, serving the Lord with humility in his sight.[1] When we spiritually 'remove our shoes' or acknowledge in our hearts that we are the Lord's and that we must serve him in the place where he has put us, that place becomes our temple and place of worship every day, whether kitchen, office or shop floor.

A prayer to say barefoot in your kitchen: Lord, I seek to serve you in all humility in the place where you have put me. Help me learn how this place can become the holy ground where I can enter your presence and serve you daily. Amen

*

Barefoot and mourning

JAMES 4:1–10 (NIV)

Purify your hearts… Grieve, mourn and wail. Change your laughter to mourning and your joy to gloom. Humble yourselves before the Lord, and he will lift you up.

When I was younger, I liked wearing very high-heeled shoes. I still have the precarious silver sandals I wore for dancing, although I can't bend my feet to get them on now! They used to make me feel like a princess, but at the end of the evening when I took them off, I was seven centimetres shorter and back down to earth. That is what happens when you 'take off your shoes' before the Lord: as I have already mentioned, you suddenly find yourself in touch with reality.

If we are committed to drawing close to God, acknowledging our workplaces as holy ground where we can meet him, we must be prepared to be brought face to face with reality: there is no more pretending. We are humbled, because when we begin to glimpse his glory and holiness we are convicted of our own guilt and unworthiness. True humility has been described as 'nothing more than an accurate self-assessment, an awareness of oneself as one really is'.[2]

We have already seen that another group of people who went barefoot in biblical times were those who mourned (2 Samuel 15:30). When we face up to the reality of ourselves, that is what we should become—humble, 'barefoot' mourners over our own shortcomings. The wonderful thing about this painful process is that the Lord Jesus Christ promises to comfort those who truly mourn (Matthew 5:4). When we humble ourselves before the Lord, swallow our pride and confess our nothingness and unworthiness, we receive that wonderful comforting forgiveness that lifts us up into closer fellowship with him.

Turn this scripture into a confessional prayer: Search me, O God, and know my heart; test me and know my anxious thoughts. See if there is any offensive way in me, and lead me in the way everlasting. Amen

PSALM 139:23–24 (NIV)

*

Barefoot and captive

ROMANS 6:15–23 (NIV)

But now that you have been set free from sin and have become slaves to God, the benefit you reap leads to holiness, and the result is eternal life.

Not only did priests and mourners go barefoot in biblical times, but, as mentioned above, captives and slaves also went without shoes. Captives being led into exile were forced to remove their shoes, and this cut them down to size: it was an act of shame and public humiliation. It also meant that escape would be painful and diffi-cult. For slaves, their bare feet were a continual reminder of their position in life at the bottom of the social order and the demand for their total obedience.

When we take off our shoes voluntarily and humble ourselves

before God, we are 'cut down to size'. Sometimes, however, rather like little children, we can't quite manage our knotted shoe fastenings and the Lord has to untangle the laces and remove our shoes for us. Unlike the victor with his captive, the Lord does not wrench off our shoes to shame and humiliate us. Our God, in Christ, kneels before us and compassionately eases off the ill-fitting footwear and bathes the sore feet with the ointment that is his Holy Spirit. By his own example, the Lord humbles us and teaches us. This doesn't mean that the removal of the stuck shoes—in other words, our proud attitude—is always totally painless; often it can leave us smarting. What freedom is felt, though, when those tight shoes are off and the ache has subsided!

When the Lord humbles us by the circumstances that he allows into our lives, and we are willing to be patient in that difficult time and learn humility from him, we become so captivated by his love that the thought of escape is difficult and painful, for to live without God at the centre of our lives is a terrible thought indeed. Humbled, captivated and freed from our sinful selves, we find that we become the willing slaves to God that Paul describes; and the desire to be obedient, and growth into holiness, are a natural consequence.

In a time of quiet, give the Lord permission to unknot and remove any ill-fitting attitudes. Ask him to begin the process today.

*

Barefoot and female

JAMES 3:13–18 (NIV)

Who is wise and understanding among you? Let him show it by his good life, by deeds done in the humility that comes from wisdom... The wisdom that comes from heaven is first of all pure; then peace-loving, considerate, submissive, full of mercy and good fruit, impartial and sincere.

I once read an article in a magazine that showed what wearing high heels does to a woman's posture—how they throw the backbone out of its natural alignment, especially if aggravated by a handbag slung over the shoulder. Tension in the spine is heightened and weaknesses accentuated. Taking off her shoes, the barefoot woman finds her natural stance, all artificial stresses and strains are removed, weaknesses are relieved and strengths are allowed to function as intended.

I am sure you can see where I am heading already! The spiritually barefoot, humble woman is unburdened from all the constraints placed on her by society and herself. She is free to stand before the Lord and allow him to make her what she should be in him and to give her the permission and authority to live it out. When we learn humility, we find our natural stance in Christ.

The verses at the start of this reading tell us that humility comes from wisdom, which is a gift of God from heaven, and we see the kind of attributes that the spiritually wise person displays. Take a moment to re-read the fruit of humility that is born from the flower of wisdom. Can you or I say that this kind of fruit is seen in our lives? Have we put ourselves in the place where God's love can touch and change us, allowing wisdom to blossom, and humility and its sister fruits to develop?

In today's world it is easy to feel that we have to conform to the image of womanhood that we see portrayed by the media and those around us. Humility, God's natural stance for women, is not fashionable, but Christ does not call us to be fashionable. He calls us to be free in him, to be what God intended.

Read and consider Proverbs 31:10–31 and compare it with our reading here. The 'wife of noble character' is considered to be the personification of wisdom, and so we could assume that her deeds spring from a humble heart. Note that humility has not shackled her, but that her work has prospered and she will receive her reward.

*

Walking barefoot

MATTHEW 11:28–30 (NIV)

'Take my yoke upon you and learn from me, for I am gentle and humble in heart, and you will find rest for your souls. For my yoke is easy and my burden is light.'

I was given these verses by a close friend on the occasion of my baptism by full immersion. That was the time when I publicly acknowledged that I was willingly taking Christ's yoke upon myself and was ready to learn from his example. The example of Jesus is one of humility that embraces servanthood, self-denial and sacrifice. Jesus doesn't bludgeon us into that mould, however; he bids us to walk beside him as he gently guides us along the way.

The yoke that Jesus was referring to in these verses was designed for two oxen to wear. The farmer would yoke an older, experienced ox on one side, and an unbroken ox on the other. Walking alongside the older animal, the younger ox would learn to walk in a straight line, not too fast and not too slow, not pulling to one side or the other but allowing the yoke to rest evenly on its shoulders so that it would not rub and chafe the skin. All the while, the older ox would be doing the brunt of the work and bearing the majority of the weight of the burdensome plough.

When we are yoked in humility with the Lord Jesus, he gently walks alongside us, showing us how to pull our weight for God's kingdom, while carrying the brunt of the load himself. Often, our pride makes us pull from side to side, race ahead or pull back from what God is calling us to do. Aligning our walk with God's will is a vital step on the path of humility. If we have answered the call of Jesus Christ and claim to live in him, we must learn to walk as Jesus walked (1 John 2:6).

> *Meditate on this verse and turn it into prayer: Trust in the Lord with all your heart and lean not on your own understanding; in all your ways acknowledge him, and he will make your paths straight.*
> PROVERBS 3:5–6 (NIV)

*

Walking in the desert

DEUTERONOMY 8:1–9 (NIV)

Remember how the Lord your God led you all the way in the desert these forty years, to humble you and to test you in order to know what was in your heart, whether or not you would keep his commands.

When we yoke ourselves to the Lord Jesus Christ and determine by his grace to learn to walk humbly in step with him, it is good to realize that humility and the formation of the heart and mind of Christ within us do not happen immediately as if by the wave of a wand. The decision to humble ourselves and to be humbled by God is only the outset of what can be a long and arduous journey.

I was speaking to a woman at church the other week who could not understand why there were so many obstacles in her life that made her Christian walk so hard. She really wanted to be like some of the older women in the fellowship, who appeared to sail through the day full of serenity and peace that obviously flowed from a deep relationship with the Lord. I was glad to be able to assure her that at least two of the women she admired had faced many struggles when they were younger, and some still struggled with hardship, but they faced it with grace that is born of patience, a gift of God's Holy Spirit.

The pressures that my friend and I, as young women with families at home, are going through now are the wilderness experiences that humble us and help us to learn how to throw ourselves on to God alone. I am sure that in ten or fifteen years' time, some of the girls who are now in the youth group will look at my friend and wish they had her spiritual character, not realizing that it was the desert experiences that made her that way!

Lord God, teach me humility by helping me to accept the demands placed on my life by your command to love others. Help me to be patient when I encounter difficulties, knowing that you call us not to give up but to persevere. Thank you that 'we are more than conquerors through him who loved us' (Romans 8:37, NIV).

*

Goodbye to all that

PHILIPPIANS 2:1–11 (NIV)

Do nothing out of selfish ambition or vain conceit, but in humility consider others better than yourselves. Each of you should look not only to your own interests, but also to the interests of others.

After I left college, I was very proud of all that I had achieved and all the knowledge I had gained. I was keen to gain more qualifications and receive the applause of the academic circles in which I moved. I very soon learned that there were a lot of people cleverer than I was, and that I had come to the limit of my understanding and abilities. It was a welcome relief to leave work and start a family.

Yet it was a struggle to learn to value myself in a domestic role and find meaning in the ordinariness of life. I had spent so many years full of 'selfish ambition and vain conceit' that finding myself as 'only a mother and a housewife' was a real blow to my pride. I became resentful and was very depressed for several years. These were my 'desert' years, during which I was reduced to the point where I was able to see that there was nothing in me or about me to be commended, except what God had done for me in Jesus Christ. I had to ask God for forgiveness for my acts of selfishness that had turned family life into a living hell.

From then on, I was able to start actively learning to put my husband's and my children's interests in their proper place in my life, rather than resenting the 'constant intrusions' and struggling to get on with my own agenda despite them. The wonderful thing about being willing to make others happy is that the time you do get to yourself is much more beneficial and productive, because your heart is nurturing the humble, compassionate attitude of Christ rather than bitterness and resentment.

Everyone naturally desires knowledge, but of what use is knowledge without the fear of God? … If you desire to know or learn anything to your advantage, then take delight in being unknown and unregarded… But always to think well and highly of others is the highest wisdom and perfection.[3]

*

Thinking clearly about yourself

GALATIANS 6:1–10 (NIV)

If anyone thinks he is something when he is nothing, he deceives himself. Each one should test his own actions. Then he can take pride in himself, without comparing himself to somebody else, for each one should carry his own load.

The more women I talk to, the more I realize that lack of self-esteem is one thing most of us hold in common, especially if we have left responsible jobs and careers to look after children, manage a house or follow a husband's career move. When we are asked what we 'do', we answer, 'I'm just a housewife' and shrink into our chairs, expecting the questioner to pass over us and talk to someone else.

We need to understand that lack of self-esteem is not the same as humility. If humility is having a realistic opinion of ourselves, accepting the place God has put us in and expecting to meet him there, then being a home-maker is as fine as being a nuclear scientist. Jeremy Taylor, the chaplain to King Charles I, wrote that humility is not the unaccepting, critical attitude that many of us hold in respect to ourselves. If you are realistic and accepting, you should 'never be ashamed of your birth, of your parents, your occupation, or your present employment, or the lowly status of any of them. When there is occasion to speak about them to others, do not be shy, but speak readily, with an indifference to how others regard you.'[4]

I think this is what Paul means in the reading here, when he says that a person can 'take pride' in themselves without comparing themselves to others. This attitude of humble indifference helps us to accept praise for something we have done and return that praise to God without taking it on board and allowing it to make us proud.

Lord, sometimes I find it difficult to accept myself as I am and my situation as it is. Help me not to be ashamed of who I am and what I do, but never let me make my own praise the intended end of anything I say or do. If I am praised, help me to have the holy indifference to return that praise to you.

An upside-down economy

JOHN 13:1–17 (NIV)

'Now that I, your Lord and Teacher, have washed your feet, you also should wash one another's feet. I have set you an example that you should do as I have done for you.'

A long time ago I went to see the film *Gandhi*. There was one part that I remember very clearly—a conversation between Gandhi and his wife. Everyone in the small community he led had to join in with all the tasks. Gandhi's wife was finding it very difficult to bring herself to accept that she should help to clean out the latrines: she belonged to a caste that did not do this job, which, in their culture, was saved for the lowest of the low. Eventually Gandhi persuaded her that honour could be found even in this most lowly of tasks, and she obediently went off to help in a job that she had previously thought she couldn't do.

I wasn't a mother when I saw that film, but once I had children that scene came to mind as I struggled with the inevitable mess that babies and toddlers produce. It was not that I thought I was above cleaning up, just that it could sometimes be such an awful job. Thinking about the film more carefully, I realized that Gandhi sent his wife to do the lowliest job—he didn't go himself—and that didn't help me to get the unpleasant tasks of motherhood completely into perspective!

How subtle a difference we see with Jesus' call to servanthood and humility. Jesus didn't tell others to go and do anything he wasn't willing to do; he was the one that did the job of the lowest of the low when he took off his disciples' sandals and washed their dirty feet. When I'm on my knees buckling small shoes, I think of Jesus, who was willing to humble himself not just by handling feet, but by dying on a cross. Then I try to see him in the person I'm serving.

Lord, help me to learn humility and service in the tasks I find difficult, never forgetting that you set us the ultimate example by giving up heaven's glory to die for us.

*

Choose the right seat

LUKE 14:1–14 (NIV)

'But when you are invited, take the lowest place, so that when your host comes, he will say to you, "Friend, move up to a better place." Then you will be honoured in the presence of all your fellow guests.'

When I was at a Christian family conference one summer, I had a reserved seat on the front row because my husband was one of the speakers. Most mornings I sat with our clingy toddler in the crèche. It rained very hard and the crèche was flooded after three days. I had not been able to attend many events, because of our toddler, so I decided to join in the worship at the beginning of the fourth morning. I made him a sandwich and strapped him in his buggy, and then pushed the buggy into the large space in front of my reserved seat. I knew buggies were a potential obstruction, but I still took it in. 'I'm exempt,' I thought. 'It won't matter, because I'm a leader's wife!' No sooner had I sat down than a steward arrived and asked me to move the buggy. In desperation I pointed to the name on my chair. It didn't work, and he signalled for reinforcements. I burst into tears and rushed out, buggy and all.

Isn't it easy to think that we are among the great because we are married to a leader—that we are above the rules? If I had, in all humility, pushed the buggy in at the back, I could have joined in the worship without the hassle that arose from my pride and presumptions. Jesus said that it was better to pray in a closet than in the open, and I am sure his words could be extended to imply that it is better to worship in humility at the back of the congregation than with subconscious superiority at the front. Who knows, if I'd done that, I might have been moved to a better place!

We can serve him when we have a position with status, and
when we do not have status. Yet, where there is a choice…
it is good to choose the lower path, because that is to
imitate Jesus more closely.[5]

*

Seeking child-like humility

MATTHEW 18:1–9 (NIV)

'I tell you the truth, unless you change and become like little children, you will never enter the kingdom of heaven. Therefore, whoever humbles himself like this child is the greatest in the kingdom of heaven.'

In the light of my confession in the previous reading, I have had to relearn the truths in the verses above. My actions and desires in wanting to worship from 'my seat' in the front row indicated that I had a jumped-up opinion of myself as the wife of the leader of a large, well-known church. Jesus said that people need to change and become like little children in order to enter his kingdom. The changing that needs to be done is not something that we can do for ourselves. It is the sort of changing that Christ does in our lives when we are born again, and is a continual learning process by his Holy Spirit every moment of every day. This total commitment to inner transformation is a constant letting go in which we see our idols successively broken and in which we cultivate an open, free response to the challenges with which God will face us.

But to be changed to become like a child? I have always struggled to understand this, as in my experience many children in our culture are anything but humble! In New Testament times, 'to be like a child' would mean to take on an attitude of great insignificance, because that is how children were considered in the social pecking order.

It is a great challenge to learn true insignificance and to become like a little child who innocently rejoices in being its own, un-complicated self. I truly struggle with this process, but I find that it can be helped along if I retreat from public visibility for a time and seek what silence and solitude I can in a family home, concentrating on performing the routine, mundane essentials of life and leaving the 'glamorous' tasks to others. Eventually true perspective is restored to my life and I find it safe to emerge again.

For prayerful meditation:
'He must become greater; I must become less.'
JOHN 3:30 (NIV)

*

The way of obedience

PHILIPPIANS 2:5–11 (NIV)

Your attitude should be the same as that of Christ Jesus: who… made himself nothing… He humbled himself and became obedient to death—even death on a cross!

Obedience and humility are inseparable virtues. It is impossible for either to function perfectly without the other, and many other virtues spring from them both. What is obedience? Many of us would have an immediately negative response, thinking that it means doing something we don't want to do!

Obedience tempered by humility is different. It is learning to say 'yes' to what the Lord wants for our lives and learning to make his will our genuine desire. How do we know what the Lord's desire for our life is? If we look at the word 'obedience', we see that it comes from the Latin *oboedire*, which has the same root as the Latin verb *audire*, 'to listen'. Literally, obedience means 'out of listening'. If we are seeking God's presence from moment to moment, we should be cultivating how to listen to him with every part of our being. Obedience is about learning (and loving) to act upon what we have heard, which can truly happen only if we have a humble attitude. The stubborn attitude hears, but hardens its heart and goes its own way. The humble attitude obeys and obeys gladly.

When I read the verse quoted, my thoughts are drawn to the garden of Gethsemane, where Jesus wrestled with God's will that he should die for us on the cross, but finally submitted himself, humbled himself and became obedient. Jesus did what he heard the Father tell him, and finished God's work. It encourages me to know that Jesus struggled like this. It helps me when I struggle over something I would rather not have to bother about, but which I know God wants me to do. It helps to know that my obedience helps God to work in and through me.

Lord, please give me an obedient heart that is willing to do what you ask of me in all humility. May that obedience spring from a sincere love of you in response to all that Christ has done for me. Amen

*

Humility and self-denial

MATTHEW 16:21–28 (NIV)

Then Jesus said to his disciples, 'If anyone would come after me, he must deny himself and take up his cross and follow me. For whoever wants to save his life will lose it, but whoever loses his life for me will find it.'

When I was a very young Christian, I was taught that true 'JOY' came by ordering your priorities: **J**esus, **O**thers, **Y**ourself. Although I am now aware that life is more complicated than I thought as an eleven-year-old, those priorities still stand; they are timeless and scriptural. As a very new Christian, I remember coming home from boarding school for the holidays and being very willing to help my mother in the kitchen, because I instinctively wanted to please Jesus.

I often wish I could regain some of the pure, uncluttered joy that I had then. Motherhood can be a Calvary road of self-denial from dawn to dusk, and often all night too. We were told at our wedding that children break the cycle of selfishness in marriage; that is very true, and I often feel that they have not just broken my selfishness, but the whole of me.

Self-denial for Jesus' sake as a mother can so easily turn into the 'doormat' syndrome. You can very easily get so tired and so over-burdened that you stop looking to Jesus for strength, and the whole of life becomes drudgery—a denial of the law of love. Self-denial for Jesus' sake does not mean the loss of our identity. It is the freedom to choose to look to others' interests as well as our own, to have the attitude 'There you are; how can I serve you?' rather than 'Here I am; notice me.' Neither is it the self-pity that encourages a perverse sense of martyrdom, manifesting itself as outward submission masking bitter inner turmoil. Conversely, self-denial treats menial chores as sacred tasks, common household objects as sacred vessels on the altar and the people we serve as if they were Christ himself.

Thank you, Lord, that the ordinary tasks we have to do every day provide us with an opportunity to crucify our selfish nature, to learn to put others first, and so keep us walking closely in step with you.

*

A humble parent

1 PETER 3:8–22 (NRSV)

Finally, all of you, have unity of spirit, sympathy, love for one another, a tender heart, and a humble mind.

I am struggling with this reading, because recently our house seems to have been a hotbed of emotion as far as the children are concerned. At the moment, the last thing our children are is harmonious, sympathetic and loving towards each other. The verse quoted here follows a long discussion by Peter on submission, and he bases his demand to his readers to submit to one another on the example of Christ (1 Peter 2:21).

Submission is impossible without the foundation of self-denial that we looked at in the previous reading. If self-denial means understanding that we don't have to have our own way, then submission is the servant heart that puts that understanding into action through the love of Jesus. That servant heart is sympathetic, loving, compassionate and humble. If all parties are operating from that framework, then living in harmony might just be possible.

I do wish I could get the children to understand these principles! I suppose that the only way is the long-term example of their parents. We all know that parents should be sympathetic, loving and compassionate—but humble? If humility is accurate self-assessment, then the humble parent is the one who knows and owns up to their faults as well as their strengths, and is willing to try to put problems right.

I have got things totally wrong with one of our children at the moment. I know the situation cannot be changed in a day and I cannot change the child concerned, but I can ask the Lord to change me and help me accept my responsibility to create the kind of environment that will allow each child to change at a rate they can cope with.

I hope that this personal example of an attempt to put humility into action will help you take this set of readings seriously. Anyone possessing humility and love has everything they need and more.

Read 1 Corinthians 13 and use it as a springboard for prayer.

---

1 W. Corswant, *A Dictionary of Life in Biblical Times*, translated by Arthur Heathcote (Hodder & Stoughton, 1960), p. 248.
2 *The Cloud of Unknowing*, H. Backhouse (ed.), Hodder & Stoughton Christian Classics, p. 38.
3 Thomas à Kempis, *The Imitation of Christ*, translated by L. Sherley-Price (Penguin, 1965), pp. 28–29.
4 Jeremy Taylor, 'The Rule & Exercise of Holy Living' (1650), in R. Foster & J. Bryan Smith (eds.), *Devotional Classics* (Hodder & Stoughton, 1993), p. 399.
5 Margaret Hebblethwaite, *Finding God in All Things* (Fount, 1987).

Lord of pots and pans

Jesus said, 'Now that I, your Lord and Teacher, have washed your feet, you also should wash one another's feet. I have set you an example that you should do as I have done for you. I tell you the truth, no servant is greater than his master...'
JOHN 13:14–16a (NIV)

In the last reflection in the previous series of Bible readings, I made the comment, 'If self-denial means understanding that we don't have to have our own way, then submission is the servant heart that puts that understanding into action through the love of Jesus.' Very fine words, but how did I try to work that out in practice?

When you are at home mothering small children full-time, the most obvious place to start is with your family; and if you struggle with domestic tasks, then self-denial and submission in that area are probably going to be your major means to developing spiritual character. Jesus humbled himself by taking off his outer clothes, wrapping a towel around his waist and washing his disciples' feet. The only way I could copy that in my situation was to take off my pride, tie an apron around my waist and learn to serve willingly and cheerfully in the kitchen for Jesus.

I have already introduced you to Brother Lawrence, the monk who worked barefoot in a monastery kitchen. My acquaintance with him led me to investigate aspects of the cloistered lifestyle more closely, because that's what I was—cloistered in my domestic situation. I came across the other monk, St Benedict, through a book by Esther de Waal that turned up in the effects of my husband's late godmother, and eventually I read his Rule for myself.[1]

Benedict helped me to take the theme of finding God in the ordinariness of my kitchen one step further, because I read that he charged the monastery cellarer to 'regard the chattels of the monastery and its whole property as if they were the sacred vessels of the altar' and that 'it is essential he should have humility… and must provide the brethren with their regular allowance of food, without fuss or keeping them waiting, so as not to make for them an occasion to sin.'[2] What was I, then, if I wasn't a sort of cellarer? I knew I had to be humble: taking my shoes off was all about that. I also had to provide food without fuss, so why not take his comments about chattels seriously too?

If the kitchen had become my holy ground, then the cooker and sink that I worked at and the table where we ate were my altar. Similarly, the pots and pans, cutlery and crockery were the holy vessels—and I should treat them as such. This was quite a tall order for me to put into practice, but I was determined to have a go. Of all the articles in my kitchen, it was the table that was to become the focus of my attention for quite a while.

Our kitchen table at the time was small; we had bought it with a tax rebate we'd received during Mark's first curacy. It seated four at a push, and there were now five of us—with a sixth on the way. Due to my exhaustion and depression, meal times had been a time of the day I dreaded. The emotional energy that I needed to expend to get three under-fives to eat seemed more than I could manage, and I was desperate to get each meal over as fast as possible. This meant that table presentation hadn't been high on my list of priorities, and, even after my healing, this hadn't been reviewed as I had so much else to work on first. So here I was, with a desire to serve in my kitchen and sanctify the means to that service, confronting a very small table that reminded me of a backlog of bad experiences. I prayed for a new and bigger table and two more chairs… and, needless to say, I got them!

At this point I came across an American book on Christian hospitality called *A House of Many Blessings*.[3] Once I'd made the necessary cultural jump, I was struck by how much effort the authors recommended putting into table presentation. My table setting style had much to be desired: while hastily throwing a meal together, I would dump the cutlery in a heap in the middle of the table, serve up the food on plates by the cooker and put them unceremoniously in front of the noisy rabble, bracing myself for the squeals of 'I don't like that' or polite silence from the other adult present. This book helped me to see that preparing a table pleasing to the eye was a quiet way of telling each family member that they were special and welcome, that care had been taken to get ready for them, and that thanks and good manners could be considered a small reward for such service.

I was game for anything at this point, but presenting a well-set table was a real pain at first. I had to figure out what would fit on the table. Although they had overtones of 'altar', flowers and candles were rejected as much for reasons of safety as of space. However, I did manage to squash in placemats, napkins, decent cutlery and china plates, real glass glasses, serving spoons and a cruet set (placed well out of the way of the one-year-old). I had to budget extra time to set the table before each meal, and the increase in washing up was horrendous. Perhaps this was one reason why I was eventually treated to a dishwasher!

As the days went by, the new routine slipped into place and small changes began to occur in the people who sat round the table. A specially laid table put us in more of a frame of mind to say grace, and the children began to remind us if we forgot. There was more inclination to try to help the children to behave well, and manners improved weekly. By the time the summer came and we spent part of our holiday in a hotel, I was not at all ashamed of their behaviour: they now knew what to do and were delighted to show us.

Putting food in serving dishes on the table may have increased the washing-up, but it gave the children the chance to see what was on offer before it ended up on their plates. I started to ask each child what they would like. They had to make choices, wait their turn, and perhaps even try food they hadn't tasted before. This was how we found out that our daughter liked chilli and curry! Being able to serve them small portions from dishes on the table, with the opportunity to have a second helping, meant that plates were emptied more often, which was important to me, as I hate waste.

Treating the meal table like an altar was paying major dividends.

My commitment to serve the family in this way also taught them to serve and help each other, to answer clearly and say 'please' and 'thank you'. Conversation began to develop during the meal, and the children learnt to take turns talking, so that sitting down at the table as a family at least once a day provided a growing forum for conversation, sharing news, discussion and planning. It was amazing how this one effort on my behalf had had so many knock-on effects: routine and structure that had begun in the kitchen spread to the rest of the house, producing a security that brought the sense of peace to our home that had been missing for many years.

The process I have described may be difficult for women older than myself to understand, because their generation had an innate structure, routine and sense of service in the home. I was brought up with this structure, but the stress, exhaustion and depression that I experienced with my first three children totally knocked that foundation away: I couldn't cope; it was all too much; just getting through the day was all I could manage. Only when I began to recuperate did I rediscover what I had lost, but I rediscovered it in the context of rebuilding my life on a spiritual foundation rather than on the foundation of expectations laid on women by the society of their time.

This spiritual experiment in the kitchen tangibly contributed to my inner peace. I don't spend as much time in the kitchen now, but I still try to keep to the basic principles I learnt during that time all those years ago. Meal times are still an opportunity to draw aside from my other preoccupations, to worship God in practical service and to show others that they are cared for and welcome.

'Serve one another in love' (Galatians 5:13b, NIV).

This is a major revision of the article 'St Benedict and Meal Times' which appeared in *Renewal* 223, December 1994, pages 30–31. Used with permission.

1 Esther de Waal, *Seeking God: the Way of St Benedict* (Fount, 1984) and *The Rule of St Benedict*, translated by Abbot Parry OSB (Gracewing, 1990).
2 *The Rule*, 31:10, 13 and 16.
3 G. Sherrer and L. Watson, *A House of Many Blessings: the Joy of Christian Hospitality* (Eagle, 1993).

A place of quiet rest

Your beauty... should be that of your inner self, the unfading beauty of
a gentle and quiet spirit, which is of great worth in God's sight.
1 PETER 3:3a–4 (NIV)

Learning to live in God's presence and cultivating humility in our
lives is the ultimate beauty treatment. This makeover doesn't work
from the outside in, but from the inside out—and it happens
gradually, without us even realizing it. What produces that in-
imitable glow is the beauty of a gentle and quiet spirit shining out
of the inner self that has cultivated an intimate relationship with
Jesus.

A quiet and gentle spirit is a product of the quietness and
gentleness found in the Lord's presence. This makes it quite natural
for the person who is seeking to live in God's presence in the
ordinariness of life to develop a desire for solitude and silence.

The following set of readings take a look at what solitude actually
is, and how solitude and silence can help us to deepen our relationship with the Lord. As mothers who are surrounded by children
and noise, it is important to understand that solitude does not
necessarily mean being alone, and silence is not necessarily the
absence of noise but an ability to let ourselves be led beside quiet
waters even when outer circumstances may seem not to permit it.

*

Solitude

PSALM 102:6–7 (NIV)

I am like a desert owl, like an owl among the ruins. I lie awake; I have become like a bird alone on a roof.

The next set of readings are going to look at solitude and silence and how, as women, we can use aspects of these disciplines to deepen our relationship with Jesus. To start with, I want to take a quick look at what is not meant by 'solitude'.

I expect, if you asked someone what they thought solitude is, they would answer, 'Being alone.' In itself, being alone is not solitude, and you don't need to be alone to enter into solitude either. The bird alone on the roof in the verse above is experiencing not solitude but loneliness and isolation. Loneliness and isolation are the result of a lack of communication between us and God or our spouse, our family members or our church fellowship. This lack of communication can produce a great sense of affliction in the life of the lonely person, which is not good for their spiritual health.

We know from the creation story in Genesis that God saw that it wasn't good for human beings to be alone. Often, the only way we can combat a sense of loneliness or isolation is to restore the lines of communication, first with God, and second with our fellow human beings. This may involve a great deal of humility: we may need to ask forgiveness from God and anyone we have offended. It may mean a great deal of self-sacrifice in learning to put the interests of others before our own so that fellowship can begin to flourish again.

Before we go further and consider what solitude is, have a quick look at your life. Are the communication lines clear and functioning between you and the Lord, between you and your family or workmates? Solitude is an attitude of inner peace. If there is unforgiveness and strife in our life, solitude can be impossible to find. Ask God's help to start putting matters right.

*

Repentance and rest

ISAIAH 30:15 (NIV)

In repentance and rest is your salvation, in quietness and trust is your strength, but you would have none of it.

Samuel Pepys, the famous 17th-century English diarist, wrote, 'My wife is troubled by her lonely life.' When my children were younger and I was stuck at home with no adult company, I too was very troubled by my lonely life. That loneliness, compounded by post-natal depression and the sheer exhaustion of having three babies in two and a half years, caused a very bitter root to spring up in my heart. I was no good on my own and I certainly was not pleasant in company.

My personal journey towards finding solitude to replace loneliness, and silence in the midst of domestic chaos, started with repentance and rest and led on into quietness and trust. I had to confess my bitterness, rage and anger towards God, my family and the church and ask for forgiveness in return. Only then was I able to experience an inner rest that allowed me to stop finding any excuse to avoid being still in God's presence. Until then, I was frightened that if I was still before God for too long, he would point out all the things I was trying to batten down and hide.

After this life-changing experience, I had about a year of quietness of heart and learning to trust. The children still prevented me from going out, and domestic life was still noisy and busy; but I was not afraid of being alone any more and was happy to stay at home with the Lord as my company. It was time to learn not to fuss unduly, but to trust God for his wisdom, strength and insight into the situations I had to cope with.

> *Meditate on these verses and turn them into prayer:*
> *'But me she forgot,' declares the Lord. 'Therefore I am now going*
> *to allure her; I will lead her into the desert and speak tenderly to*
> *her. There I will give her back her vineyards, and will make the*
> *Valley of Achor [trouble, anguish, crying] a door of hope.*
> *There she will sing as in the days of her youth.'*
> HOSEA 2:13b–15a (NIV)

*

God—our 'sole-attitude'

PSALM 27:4–5 (NIV)

One thing I ask of the Lord, this is what I seek: that I may dwell in the house of the Lord all the days of my life, to gaze upon the beauty of the Lord and to seek him in his temple. For in the day of trouble he will keep me safe in his dwelling; he will hide me in the shelter of his tabernacle.

I have struggled for quite a while to decide how I can describe or define 'solitude'. I have talked about how solitude is not being alone in the sense of being lonely, but solitude does need times of being alone if it is to be cultivated. I think Richard Foster was given great insight to call solitude 'the portable sanctuary of the heart'.[1] It is the inner attentiveness to Jesus that we carry with us through the day— God's gift of grace to us when we discipline ourselves to practise living constantly in his presence.

Solitude is about being in right relationship with God, about resting in him. It is the call to 'abide' that Jesus makes to his disciples; it is the knowing of God in the depths of our being, which is itself the work of the Holy Spirit. Solitude is the relinquishing of our own will in favour of God's will; it is being able to hear God's gentle whisper and having the innate desire to obey without question. Solitude is the ability of the heart and mind to be so lost in love for the Saviour that you desire only to gaze and gaze upon him.

At first, my experiences of real solitude were none too frequent, but once a way has been established into the portable sanctuary of your heart, successive visits become easier. In 'the day of trouble' (and all carers have those days), we can take refuge there as we deal with the demands of those around us.

Lord, make my heart into a portable sanctuary, so that I can retreat and rest there, and gaze on you, even when I am surrounded by noise and dealing with chaos.

*

Come up here

REVELATION 4:1–2 (NIV)

After this I looked, and there before me was a door standing open in heaven. And the voice I had first heard speaking to me like a trumpet said, 'Come up here…' At once I was in the spirit, and there in heaven stood a throne, with one seated on the throne!

In the previous reading, we thought a little bit about gazing on the Lord, and how our hearts can become a portable sanctuary where we can do just that. In the temple in Jerusalem during biblical times, the innermost sanctuary was called the holiest place; it was considered to be the earthly counterpart of God's throne in heaven. Only the priests were allowed to enter there, and then only once a year on the Day of Atonement. Such was the privilege of being able to enter God's earthly presence that the priests used to draw lots to see who would go in.

There is no equivalent physical temple for us to enter today, but the New Testament tells us that we ourselves are the temple of God's Holy Spirit. In the inner silence of our hearts, our portable sanctuary, we can enter the holiest place of God's presence and enjoy, in solitude, beholding the throne of God in devotional prayer, just as is described in the verses above.

If you can find even ten minutes to yourself when the children are sleeping or everyone is out, you may find it helpful to read Revelation 4, to help you practise coming into the presence of God, the Most Holy One, and gazing on him in his throne room in pure adoration. Sit comfortably and read the passage slowly, using all your senses to enter into the scene described: see the colours, bask in the light, hear the sounds, smell the incense and worship the Lord as the Holy Spirit leads you.

Done often enough, this meditative exercise can develop in us a contemplative heart full of pure, unaided adoration of God.

Lord, help me to learn how to lose myself in you, so that, like Jacob, I can say, 'How awesome is this place! This is none other than the house of God, and this is the gate of heaven' (Genesis 28:17, NIV).

*

After the fire

1 KINGS 19:9–13a (NIV)

*The Lord said, 'Go out and stand on the mountain in the presence
of the Lord, for the Lord is about to pass by.' Then a great and power-
ful wind tore the mountains apart... After the wind there was an
earthquake... After the earthquake came a fire... And after the fire
came a gentle whisper. When Elijah heard it, he pulled his cloak over
his face and went out and stood at the mouth of the cave.*

In this reading, we are leaving the inner sanctuary of the temple and
the throne room of heaven and coming back down to earth. Elijah the
prophet has travelled to the mountain of the Lord to hide from his
enemies, the same mountain where God appeared to Moses in the
burning bush. God asks Elijah why he is hiding there. When Elijah
answers him, the Lord then replies that Elijah must come out of the
cave and stand on the mountain, for his presence is about to pass by.

The power of the earthquake, wind and fire must have been
awesome. Elijah must have been afraid; but somehow he knew that
the Lord was not present in them. Only when he heard the 'still
small voice' (RSV) did Elijah come out of the cave with his face
covered. The presence in that gentle whisper must have been very
distinctive for Elijah to distinguish it from what had come before.
The Lord then asks Elijah again why he is hiding, and Elijah gives
the same reply. This time God tells Elijah to go back the way he
came and gives him instructions... and Elijah doesn't object. There
must have been a life-changing power in that gentle whisper of the
Lord's presence, which helped Elijah to see his answer to God's
question in a new perspective.

When we enter the presence of God in stillness and solitude,
and hear his gentle whisper, he can change our perspective on the
problems we are hiding from. Then he sends us back to the place

we ran from, with new instructions and new confidence in what he can do.

> *Lord, help me recognize your gentle whisper in the storms that rage around me. Strengthen and instruct me so that I can face the problems I would rather run and hide from. Amen*

*

The sacrament of the present moment

PSALM 90:1–12 (NIV)

For a thousand years in your sight are like a day that has just gone by, or like a watch in the night... Teach us to number our days aright, that we may gain a heart of wisdom.

Life today is not just crowded with people and noise; it is also very rushed and stressed. All day long we catch ourselves saying things like, 'Hurry up, you'll be late for school'; 'We'll take the car, there's no time to walk'; and so it goes on. Before we know it, the day has rushed by and we are left in an exhausted heap, wondering quite what we have accomplished.

Slowing down the pace of our lives can help predispose our inner selves to solitude and silence. Rather than racing thoughtlessly from one task to the next, worried about how to fit everything into the day, it is much more beneficial to realize that the trivial things that happen to us in each moment are ordered by God and are therefore the best that can happen—divine appointments in which we meet God in the little things of life. In this respect, I love the observation of J.P. Caussade: 'The more we apply ourselves to our little task, so simple, so hidden, so contemptible as its outward appearance may be, the more God diversifies and beautifies it.'[2]

I was struggling through the bedtime routine the other night, determined to have some time to myself. It was hopeless: you just know when a baby is not going to settle quickly. In the end I abandoned myself to the Lord's will for that moment and enjoyed some time of lying quietly next to the baby as he drifted into sleep. I listened to God's Spirit whispering to my heart about how the Father cradles us in his arms and gives us comfort and rest.

Lord, help me to slow down today and constantly ask you what you want me to do. Help me to hear your voice in every situation. Beautify and diversify every task I perform, however lowly. Amen

*

Equanimity

ECCLESIASTES 3:1–14 (NIV)

There is a time for everything, and a season for every activity under heaven.

'Equa-what?' Equanimity basically means 'having an equal mind', 'learning to hold all things in balance', or knowing that there is 'a season for every activity under heaven' and trying to apply that to our lives. Why should this matter so much in relation to perfecting solitude and inner silence?

If a person, or even a family, can establish a firm but flexible daily, weekly and monthly routine that adjusts with the seasons and provides a time for all that is necessary, the stress and strain that the person or the family members usually experience can be significantly reduced. This can be particularly effective if passive and active tasks are carefully interspersed and time is made for personal space. Against this background of stability and relative predictability, it is much easier to cultivate inner silence and solitude than against a raging sea of ever-fluctuating chaos. How do I know this? Because I have tried it.

When the family and I know what is going on and what is likely to happen, then peace reigns in our house, even if it is the 'noisy peace' of happily playing children. Then I am more likely to be able to make my 'sole-attitude' one that is attentive towards Jesus than when the storm waters are raging around me. For example, although it may sound quite old-fashioned, when our children were small they had to play quietly in their rooms after lunch at the weekends. This helped to balance the activity of the morning and enabled them to calm down and learn to be happy with their own company, and eventually with the Lord's. It also gave their exhausted parents time to gather breath for the next sprint!

Now that the children are older, routines for homework and social activities outside the home have taken priority—but these have been laid on the foundations of stability and responsibility that we instilled in them earlier in their lives, and there is relative peace in the house.

Take a look at your routine. What needs balancing, cutting short, cutting out or slotting in? Warning: make changes slowly with your spouse's knowledge and approval!

Meaningful conversation

MATTHEW 12:36 (NIV)

Jesus said, 'But I tell you that men will have to give account on the day of judgment for every careless word they have spoken.'

It can be very difficult to be quiet in public. As a vicar's wife, I often have to make conversation with people I don't know terribly well. To cover my awkwardness and shyness, I often ramble on about all sorts of incidents that are not really necessary to mention. Then I come home and feel quite foolish, just the way Thomas à Kempis did when he wrote:

Often I wished I had remained silent... Why is it that we are so ready to chatter and gossip with each other, when we so seldom return to silence without some injury to our conscience? We think to find consolation in this manner... but this outward consolation is no small obstacle to inner and divine consolation.[3]

We spend a lot of time in chatter because we are constantly trying to make sure that people don't misunderstand us. We may offer information because we are trying to adjust other people's perception of us, because we want to be liked and accepted, or because we want to manipulate and control a person or situation. We do all this because of our hidden insecurities and fears—low self-esteem, loneliness, lack of confidence.

If we are trying to be attentive in our hearts and minds towards Jesus, then being quiet in public should become easier with time, as our confidence becomes rooted in our relationship with Jesus. When we are at peace with him and ourselves, we don't need to worry about what others might be thinking of us, and the need to chatter is reduced.

It can be difficult to relinquish control to Jesus and risk being misunderstood by becoming a person of few words—but it is worth a try.

Lord, increase your peace in my heart, still my turmoil and heal my insecurities, so that the words I speak may reflect your love.

*

A quiet house

PROVERBS 17:1; 21:9; 14:1 (NIV)

Better a dry crust with peace and quiet than a house full of feasting, with strife… Better to live on a corner of the roof than share a house with a quarrelsome wife.

The wise woman builds her house, but with her own hands the foolish one tears hers down.

One thing that is conducive to producing inner silence is outer silence. Children can be very noisy, but wives and mothers can be just as bad. I remember apologizing to some neighbours once about the amount of noise the children made in the garden. 'Don't worry,' they replied, 'all we ever hear is you!' I was horrified!

Joking aside, this sort of noise—incessant nagging and over-loud disciplining—is not constructive. It is foolish behaviour that 'tears down your own house' and could drive your husband to live on a corner of the roof or, rather, to stay as long as possible at work to avoid the tension. This sort of behaviour also exasperates and embitters children, and eventually you hear the same attitudes in their conversations with each other.

I often catch myself saying to the children, 'If you can't say anything nice, don't say anything at all.' How I could do with taking my own advice!

What makes us nag? What makes me nag? I usually begin to be over-verbal when I am stressed because there is too much to fit into the time available and the balancing act has gone wrong. One example is when I take on too much paid work because I want us to be able to live on more than 'a dry crust' and to be able to feast a bit. But look at the cost! Peace and quiet is much more valuable. It is much more desirable to provide the family with an atmosphere of peace and quiet in which they can thrive, even if tea turns out to be beans on toast by the end of the month.

Teach me, and I will be quiet; show me where I have been wrong.
JOB 6:24 (NIV)

*

Silence in heaven

REVELATION 8:1–5 (NIV)

There was silence in heaven for about half an hour.

The last couple of readings have looked at tempering the kind of noise we make at home and in the community, and reducing it as necessary. But what about complete silence? Have you ever thought of that?

Practising complete silence can give us a chance to hear God's voice more clearly. When we are silent, we may not be talking outwardly, but inwardly we can converse with ourselves and with the Lord. There is time to lay our problems and struggles before him and be open and quiet enough to hear his honest solutions.

It is fair to say that complete silence is not something we can readily experience these days, even when we are alone. Alone in the so-called silence of my kitchen late at night, I can hear cars, the central heating, clocks and domestic appliances—at least four—and a snoring dog. During the day, I have the added clamour of children's videos, PCs, phones and doorbells ringing. Finding a pool of silence seems impossible.

But there are snatches of silence that occur during our day— minute retreats when we can commit ourselves to communing with God in our hearts. For me, these moments may be walking back from school having dropped off the children, walking the dog round the common, standing at the sink or working in the garden.

Until recently, I was convinced that these little oases were enough, but as I experience more solitude and silence, I realize that it is important to make time to be silent and *still*, so that we can focus our attention properly. We may not be able to do this all at once, but it is something to work towards over the course of time. When there was silence in heaven for half an hour, the angels didn't carry on with what they were doing but were silent and still before God—and that is an intimacy worth aiming for.

Lord, show me where to stop and rest. Point out the quiet places in my day that I can use to talk with you. Teach me how to be silent and still in your presence.

*

A solitary place

MARK 1:35–37 (NIV)

Very early in the morning, while it was still dark, Jesus got up, left the house and went off to a solitary place, where he prayed. Simon and his companions went to look for him, and when they found him, they exclaimed: 'Everyone is looking for you!'

The best reason for disciplining ourselves to make time to be alone with the Father is because Jesus set us an example. Here we see Jesus getting up early to find somewhere quiet to be alone with God, even though he knew people would come looking for him.

Before I had four small children, getting up early to spend time with God was not too much of a problem. Morning feeds and colicky babies cut across all that. Any regular devotional time went out of the window and I found myself with ever-increasing feelings of guilt that I wasn't able to have my half-hour with the Lord before the day started. People weren't just looking for me, they were permanently attached!

When we are bound by habit and law, rather than being open to flexibility and grace, breaking free and finding a creative alternative can be extremely difficult; and this applies to finding time to be with God. If we suffer from this condition, which is often called 'hardening of the *ought*-eries', what we need to cure it is the understanding that God wants us to spend time with him and that it doesn't matter whether it is morning, noon or night—as long as we do it! Allowing God's love and grace to flow through us in this way will soon soften us up again.

Take ten minutes to review your week. See where you could slot in a short time each day to spend time praying and meditating on God's word without having to leave the house so that a search party is organized to find you!

Lord, I want to spend time with you in 'the secret place'. Give me the determination and discipline to make that work in my own particular life circumstances.

*

The prayer of quiet

MATTHEW 26:36–45 (NIV)

Then Jesus went with his disciples to a place called Gethsemane, and he said to them, 'Sit here while I go over there and pray.' ... Then he returned to his disciples and found them sleeping. 'Could you men not keep watch with me for one hour?' he asked Peter.

Sitting still in silence with God can be very daunting if we are not used to it, or if we are out of practice. I'm sure I'm not the only one who's sat down with good intentions, only to wake up again an hour or so later. What is encouraging is that it is not only busy mums who find it hard to spend time focusing on the Lord; even those who have committed themselves to a life of devotion find it difficult.

St Teresa of Avila struggled for many years to concentrate her mind during prayer. As a result of her experience, she made some useful suggestions that can help us to focus on God in quietness.

My favourite suggestion of hers is to imagine Christ's presence. She used to imagine she was keeping Jesus company in prayer in the garden of Gethsemane because, as she says, 'It seemed to me that his being alone and afflicted like a person in need made it possible for me to approach him.'[4] She called it 'the prayer of quiet'—a kind of prayer in which the Lord gives us his peace through his presence.

Other people find that lighting a candle is a useful aid. It makes a physical signal that the time of quiet has begun and gives the eye something to concentrate upon, with the effect of stilling the mind—but you have to be very careful if you've got young children around!

Find some time and space to be quiet and unhurried before God.
Read the story of Jesus in Gethsemane and imagine the scene.
How close do you feel you can get before you kneel and keep watch
with him? Are you able to move closer the longer you are there?
What do Christ's words of prayer make you feel? How do you
respond? What is God speaking into your heart?

*

Beat the retreat?

SONG OF SONGS 2:10–13 (NIV)

My lover spoke and said to me, 'Arise, my darling, my beautiful one, and come with me.'

If you catch the solitude and silence bug seriously, you may want to get away from all the noise and bustle of the family home and see if you can cope with 'real' solitude and silence in a retreat house.

I decided to try this the week before our fourth baby was born: it would be my last chance to get away for a long time. I arranged to leave the older children at home with my husband and went on a 48-hour silent, guided retreat at a nearby Christian retreat centre. I just wanted to get away to be with Jesus and listen to what he had to say to me.

I was relieved when the silence actually began, because it forced people to stop commenting on my enormous pregnant shape. To begin with, silence was hard to adjust to, but by the next morning I knew that we were all beginning to tune in. I can only describe it as like being at a spiritual detoxification unit where all the stresses, strains, concerns and worries of everyday life were drained away and replaced by the loving silence of God's presence.

One of the exercises we had to do was to fold a piece of A4 paper into six squares and draw on four of them a picture representing key stages in our spiritual journey to date. Square five was for what God was saying to us that day, and the last square was for a personal prayer for the future.

My square for the present day contained a drawing of a bouquet of 'bridal wreath' (*Spirea*) from the retreat house garden. God had spoken to me through the passage above from Song of Songs and made promises for my future. When we give the Lord space to meet with us, he does so in a very special and personal way, and we return to the rest of life inspired and refreshed.

Try the A4 paper exercise for yourself. Keep it somewhere safe but to hand as a reminder of God's faithfulness.

*

The voice of the heart

ZEPHANIAH 3:17 (NIV)

The Lord your God is with you, he is mighty to save. He will take great delight in you, he will quiet you with his love, he will rejoice over you with singing.

It is impossible to do justice to the topic of solitude and silence in so few readings, but I hope that this series has whetted your appetite to try to experience God in new and deeper ways in your own situation.

I chose the verse above as a word of encouragement on which to end this chapter. Making time to be with God can seem an impossible task for many women in the busy lives they lead. What we must remember is that God is on our side in relation to this. He doesn't work against us, but for us—because he loves us deeply. Often we are our own stumbling-blocks, thinking that we have to do or achieve certain spiritual standards before we can have a deep experience of God. This is not the case. God will meet us right where we are if we give him the slightest chance.

Jesus was willing to redeem and save us. He did this because we are precious and of great concern to him, and he is longing to see us grow up in the love that the Father offers us. It is the realization of God's love that will lead us gently into those quiet places where we can meet with him. Because he loves us, the Lord shows us where and when to stop and rest (Psalm 139:2–4, NIV), but we are the ones who have to make the decision to stop and rest, rather than busying ourselves with unnecessary tasks.

If we do draw aside and allow him to quieten us with his love, in our hearts we will hear the Lord rejoicing over us with singing, like a bridegroom rejoices over his bride (Isaiah 62:5).

> 'It is love which is the voice of the heart. Love God and you will always be speaking to him… Ask God to open your heart and kindle in it a spark of his love, then you will begin to understand what praying means.'[5]

Jean-Nicholas Grou. -18 'How to pray?

---

1 R. Foster, *A Celebration of Discipline* (Hodder & Stoughton, 1982).

2 J.P. Caussade, *Self-abandonment to Divine Providence*, translated by A. Thorold (Burns, Oates & Washbourne Ltd., 1952).

3 à Kempis, *The Imitation of Christ*, pp. 36–37.

4 Quoted in Jane Keiller, *Patterns of Prayer* (Daybreak, 1989), ch. 8.

5 Jean-Nicholas Grou (1730–1803), *How to Pray*, translated by Joseph Dalby (James Clarke & Co., 1955), quoted in Foster and Smith (eds.), *Devotional Classics*, p. 206.

A balanced life

God is not a God of disorder but of peace.
1 CORINTHIANS 14:33a

We've just been focusing on quietness and how that might be possible in a life filled with the clamour of young children. When I think about quietness, I have always been drawn to a verse of a well-known hymn:

> *Drop thy still dews of quietness,*
> *'til all our strivings cease,*
> *take from our souls the strain and stress,*
> *and let our ordered lives confess*
> *the beauty of thy peace.*
>
> JOHN GREENLEAF WHITTIER (1807–92)

In this hymn, quietness is dependent on the Lord teaching us how to stop striving so that we might be rid of the strain and stress we carry around with us. Although it says that we can achieve this by allowing ourselves to be filled with more of what I can only assume is a metaphor for the Holy Spirit, it is interesting that it mentions an ordered lifestyle as the witness to change in our inner being.

I have learned enough about the dynamics of spiritual life to know that if we allow the Lord to drop his quietness into our lives, it will produce a certain level of order in the way we live, as a result of knowing his peace. I also know that if we actively nurture the order that God's quietness is beginning to develop in our lives, the quietness will begin to grow too. This isn't something you can measure and prove, other than through your own experience. In fact, all the disciplines and attributes that I touch on in this book are interconnected: developing one automatically causes growth in all the others.

Wanting to experience more of the Lord through practising his presence and cultivating inner solitude and silence, I now thought it a good idea to work on the practical end of the spectrum and see what I could do to bring more order into my life. You can read about the beginnings of that quest in the chapter entitled 'Lord of pots and pans', but I didn't simply want peace, quiet and order in the kitchen—it had to pervade my whole life.

I took another look at St Benedict. It seemed that he was very concerned to see order in the lives of his monks, but he preferred to call it 'balance'. I tend to agree that 'balance' is a preferable word: it lacks the sense of compulsion that you hear in the word 'order'. I'm no good at being compelled; it makes me want to dig in my heels and resist! I wondered if the balancing of the cloistered day might have anything to say about bringing God's order into my busy daily life. After all, 'God is not a God of disorder but of peace' (1 Corinthians 14:33a, NIV).

I found that the monks' day was taken up with three kinds of activity—the work of God (four hours), the work of the hands (six hours) and the work of the mind (four hours). These chunks of time were woven together so that each kind of activity followed another repeatedly in a rhythmical balance throughout the day—rather like plaiting a triple-braided cord. It is interesting to read in Ecclesiastes 4:12 (NIV) that 'a cord of three strands is not quickly broken'. This is usually interpreted as referring to God cementing a marriage relationship, but it could easily be understood as referring to a life in which the use of body, mind and spirit are balanced, so that it resists the stress and strain better than a life that has one strand missing or one strand thicker or thinner than the others.

The work of God, or prayer, is obviously the most important thread. Stopping at points of the day to pray should, however, be the vocalization of something that is going on in our lives all the time. I have included some Bible readings on my thoughts about prayer later in this book, so here I shall discuss only a few practicalities.

Prayer at regular intervals during the day would have been too much to ask of myself as the mother of small children. Contemporary lifestyles are such that even praying together as a couple or as a family unit is quite a struggle. The hardest thing for adults with young families is finding time alone with God— someone always needs you—but adding the visible thread of prayer to an ordered life is the key element to finding true peace.

During my first years at boarding school, a morning quiet time was an imposed part of the daily routine: a bell rang and we sat in our beds to read the Bible and pray for ten minutes. There was no way I could do that in the morning when the children were small. The temptation in that kind of situation is to give up our devotions altogether. Then we enter the spiral of guilt that prevents us from trying to enter God's presence because we think he isn't interested in failures. Stop! Realize that God knows what we are going through and loves us no less for our 'failings'.

Angela Ashwin encourages the busy mother to recognize moments of quiet for what they are and grab them when they happen, despite the debris that may be demanding attention.[1] During these fleeting spaces, we can sit down and vocalize the silent stream of prayer on which we are learning to build our lives. It's impossible to predict when these quiet spaces might happen, and it takes practice to recognize them. If one child is at nursery and the baby dozes off in his buggy, there is a tendency to race around doing the thousand jobs you think you can't do when the baby is awake and the toddler at home.

Try hard to ask the Lord to show you when to stop and rest (Psalm 139:2). It can be enough to sit back exhausted, close your eyes, open your hands and heart and allow God's Spirit to pray quietly in you and through you. Speaking Jesus' name softly and repetitively can help to calm and focus the mind until we are quiet enough to lay our burdens at his feet. It is then that he drops the 'still dews of quietness' and refreshes us enough to return to the manual jobs we have to do.

We all know enough about the 'work of the hands'; there is more than enough of that when you have a young family. There are ways to sanctify those tasks: cultivating a servant heart is one way—doing everything for Jesus, looking for the face of Christ in your demanding child or the unexpected visitor. Slowing down and developing a sense of the moment can make us more aware of the presence of God in us and around us. Dressing a child, buttoning coats, peeling potatoes—consciously try to slow each job down, be aware of the physical action with all five senses and turn it into a breathed prayer of thanks and blessing.

Working with the hands also gives us an opportunity to get to know ourselves and examine our lives. The rhythmic nature of gardening, ironing, washing windows, baking or craft work provides time for the things deep in our subconscious to surface naturally, and provides space for us to bring them before the Lord. Even five minutes of uninterrupted dough-kneading while your toddler cuts out pastry shapes provides enough time for inner communion with the Holy Spirit. Be creative; think how you can make this work for you while making sure your children are happy and safe.

'The work of the mind' includes reading and study. For monks, that would have been devotional reading. There's nothing stopping you doing some devotional reading either, but any time reading anything is a precious commodity when you are at home with little ones. Young mums often say that they feel completely brain-dead, but it pays to try to keep the little grey cells ticking over, even at a very low level. Not only does it help to produce a healthy balance in your life, but it keeps your mind fit for the time you may need to pick up your career again.

So, there you have a few thoughts on spiritual balance—a time for everything, and every thing in God's time—a way to help cultivate the inner peace that we so long for in domestic chaos. Developing balance takes time and patience but pays great dividends. Try to find time to stop and think how you are weaving your braided cord.

Thoughts on 'balance' in the Benedictine life were based on Esther de Waal, *Seeking God—the way of St Benedict* (Fount, 1984), ch, 6, and Esther de Waal's Preface in *The Rule of St Benedict* (Gracewing, 1990).

Parts of this article were taken from 'Spiritual Order in Domestic Chaos', which appeared in *Renewal* 217, June 1994, pages 28–29. Used with permission.

1   A. Ashwin, *Patterns not Padlocks* (Eagle, 1992).

A heart at peace

May the God of peace… equip you with everything good for doing his will, and may he work in us what is pleasing to him, through Jesus Christ.
HEBREWS 13:20–21 (NIV)

Solitude and silence go together like peace and quiet, so it seems natural to move on to spend some time thinking about how we can allow the Lord's peace to reign in our hearts, and how we can strengthen our trust in him so that it gives us the inner quiet we long for.

Although peace and trust strengthen our inner being, it's great to read here that peace is given to us in order to equip us to do God's will. That means that inner peace should result in outward activity performed with God-given confidence. It is not an excuse to withdraw into introspective passivity. In actively following the Lord's will in the practical details of life, we learn to flex our spiritual muscles and trust him for the strength and inspiration to tackle the issues that we come up against day by day.

A heart at peace gives life to the body (Proverbs 14:30), and that's what Jesus came to give us—life in all its abundance. If you are struggling at home with young ones, life may not feel at all abundant; but when we make peace, God's peace, with our situation, he can breathe his life into us and the nitty-gritty of the daily round loses the irksomeness it had before.

*

Peace and salvation

ROMANS 5:1–10

So now, since we have been made right in God's sight by faith in his promises, we can have real peace with him because of what Jesus Christ our Lord has done for us.

We all long for peace. One of the best-selling books in England in 1999 was *The Little Book of Calm*.[1] This tells me that people are desperate for any advice that might offer the hope of some peace and tranquillity in their lives. The advice given in this book ranges from the ridiculous—'Try wearing Donald Duck underwear'—to the sublime—'If you have a faith, spend some time in prayer!' I haven't any intention of trying the first, but the second offers the only real hope for anyone to find peace.

When we take time out to pray, we enter God's presence, and in the sight of a holy God we realize what causes our absence of peace—primarily our sin and secondarily our anxieties. If the primary cause of lack of peace in our lives is sin, what can be done about it?

The only thing that can be done with our wrong thoughts, words and deeds is to own up to them before God and say sorry. God the Father can then forgive us because Jesus Christ took the punishment we deserved, by dying on the cross. We then experience the deep inner peace of knowing that we are right in God's sight.

People do not experience the peace that Christ offers us because they live in denial that they fall short of God's standards. Let's spend a little time today taking stock of our lives and asking God to forgive us for those things that rob us of the peace that is rightfully ours in Christ.

May the God of peace himself make you entirely pure and devoted to God; and may your spirit and soul and body be kept strong and blameless... God, who called you to become his child, will do all this for you, just as he promised.

1 THESSALONIANS 5:23–24

*

Peace and persecution

MATTHEW 10:26–38

If anyone publicly acknowledges me as his friend, I will openly acknowledge him as my friend before my Father in heaven... Don't imagine that I came to bring peace to the earth! No, rather, a sword.

It is easy to think that because Jesus came into the world to bring peace between God and humanity, he will automatically bring peace between us as individuals. Unfortunately this is not so. As soon as we stand up and announce that we belong to Christ, we can expect opposition rather than goodwill, and usually first from our own extended household.

It is the inner peace we have in God through Christ that gives us the love and forbearance to live with such adversity. This is the true test of peace, because it is relatively easy to live peaceably with those who think as we do, as opposed to those who do not.

Jesus tells us to love our enemies and to pray for those who persecute us so that we may be true sons (or daughters) of our Father in heaven (Matthew 5:44–45). Peter encourages us to be happy if we are insulted for being a Christian, because 'when that happens the Spirit of God will come upon you with great glory' (1 Peter 4:14).

Let's spend some time today praying for those who make our lives difficult because of our faith. Ask God to bless them and grant them an understanding of his peace. If we need to ask forgiveness from God for thoughts we have harboured in our hearts against these people, now is the time to remove that barrier to the work of the Spirit of peace.

> *Make me a channel of your peace;*
> *where there is hatred let me bring your love.*
>
> FRANCIS OF ASSISI (1181–1226)

*

Peace and possibilities

ROMANS 12:9–21 (LB)

Never pay back evil for evil. Do things in such a way that everyone can see you are honest through and through. Don't quarrel with anyone. Be at peace with everyone, so far as it depends on you.

When I was at school, there was a girl in my year who really did not like me. I hadn't done anything to upset her, but she was the kind of person who made you feel you needed to apologize just for breathing. When you are living in a dormitory with such a person, it tests your Christian love and desire for peace to the limit... and everyone else is watching to check up what difference your faith in Christ makes in the situation.

I used to hang on to the passage above for dear life, and pursue peace as far as was possible. That is all you can do! If the other person won't budge, there remains an uneasy truce, but you know that in Christ you have done all you possibly can.

Doing all you possibly can do demands extreme sacrifices. You find yourself apologizing for things that you know were not your fault in order to defuse explosive situations. You can find yourself altering your behaviour within reasonable boundaries so as not to upset the person concerned. It can mean sending a note and some flowers, writing a long-overdue letter, going that extra mile.

There is a very thin line, however, between this type of humble submission and setting oneself up as a target for plain abuse. I personally feel that if a situation veers to the latter, avoidance is the only tactic worth considering.

Lord, help us to try to live in peace with others, even if we have to run after that peace to catch and hold it. Show us what we must do with difficult people, asking you for the strength to bear suffering for your sake. Amen

*

Peace and quietness

1 TIMOTHY 2:1–15

Live in peace and quietness, spending... time in godly living and thinking much about the Lord. This is good and pleases God our Saviour... God sent pain and suffering to women when their children are born, but he will save their souls if they trust in him, living quiet, good and loving lives.

When you mention the word 'peace', the next word that springs to mind is 'quiet'. If you ask many men, the one thing that you can pretty much guarantee is that they will not describe women as 'quiet'! According to a TV programme I saw once, a woman's brain is designed to natter, and a man's is not.[2] The problem for us is learning the right time to be quiet and the right time to speak up. A lot of the 'peace' in our house is ruined not just by clamorous children but by the noisy mother trying to quieten them.

Quietness is not just about learning to refrain from speaking at the wrong moment. Outward quietness springs from a quiet spirit, a heart that rests in Jesus. Jesus says that you can tell what is in a person's heart by what comes out of their mouth (Luke 6:45). So often, my words are a reflection of inner turmoil and struggle rather than the peace that Jesus gives.

The verses above encourage us to 'live in peace and quietness' so that we can spend time in 'godly living and thinking about the Lord' because this 'pleases God our Saviour'. The converse is also true, that if we spend our time with our minds fixed on Jesus rather than on the daily problems that stir up unrest in our hearts, what comes out of our mouths will be more in keeping with what pleases the Lord, and that will have a knock-on effect on the quality of peace in our homes.

*Lord, forgive me for the times when I have ruined the peace
in my home and the hearts of my family by the thoughtlessness,
quantity and noisiness of my words. I know that they spring from a
heart that does not rest in you. Help me to take my eyes away from
the problems I wrestle with and look only to you.
In doing so, grant me your peace. Amen.*

*

Peace and possessions

MATTHEW 6:19–24

*Don't store your profits here on earth where they can erode away or may
be stolen. Store them in heaven where they will never lose their value,
and are safe from thieves.*

I opened a drawer in the laundry room this afternoon and discovered that a mouse had chewed its way through a whole pile of towelling nappies, from top to bottom, leaving a pile of droppings at the base of the hole. It made me think about the work we bring upon ourselves and the peace we lose because we are burdened by caring for all our possessions, especially what we don't actually need.

One thing we can do to make sure we are filled with peace, not stress, is to choose to own less rather than more. The more we have, the more we have to keep clean, organize and worry about losing by our own carelessness or the malicious intent of others. It robs us of much peace. Jesus tells us to store our treasure in heaven where it is safe. Then our minds can be fixed on him and be at peace.

Shedding a multitude of possessions is not easy and often cannot be done all at once. I have found that it is best to go through one room at a time and ask, 'Have I used this in the last year, will I use it in the next year, is it a family heirloom or a gift from one of the children or my husband?' If the answer is a fourfold 'No!' then the item is in serious risk of being disposed of. The less we have to look after, the more time we have to do what lies close to our hearts.

Lord, you know how much I desire to have a nice home and nice clothes and to surround myself with material things. Forgive me for feeling that this will bring me earthly security, and help me to reorder my priorities so that my heart may be at peace. Amen

*

Peace and equanimity

LUKE 10:38–42

But Martha was the jittery type, and was worrying over the big meal she was preparing.

This translation makes Martha sound just like me! One week not so long ago, I had 103 people to entertain in the course of four different events, and did I worry about it! What were we going to eat? How would I get the tables, chairs and crockery arranged? How could I do all that shopping and not spend every day at the superstore? How could I do all that cooking? I had commandeered help, but I still had to orchestrate it!

As you can imagine, there had not been much peace in the house that week. I had allowed myself to take my eyes off the purpose of the events—to focus on our guests—and got embroiled in the preparation. I had lost my equanimity, which is literally 'a balanced mind at peace'. Jesus says to Martha and me, 'Dear friend, you are so upset over all these details! There is really only one thing worth being concerned about' (vv. 41–42). That 'one thing' is knowing when to sit still and be with Jesus and let the many details recede into their proper place.

Equanimity, or its more fashionable synonym 'serenity', is the product of allowing Jesus into our diaries on a daily, weekly, monthly and annual basis, asking him, 'What do you want me to do?' Then we will have adequate time to be with God, ourselves and our families, and to spend that time peacefully, knowing that we are flowing with God's will.

Lord, forgive me for allowing myself to sink in so much unnecessary activity and worry. Order my steps, so that I might do only what you want me to do. Help me prayerfully to consider the demands on my time and give me the courage to say 'No' when necessary. Amen

*

Peace and humility

ROMANS 12: 1–16

Don't copy the behaviour and customs of this world, but be a new and different person with a freshness in all you do and think. Then you will learn from your own experience how his ways will really satisfy you... Don't try to act big. Don't try to get into the good books of important people, but enjoy the company of ordinary folk. And don't think you know it all!

These verses talk about living in humility—accepting God's plan and place for us rather than striving to attain status and recognition in the world's eyes by secular means. In the West we are constantly under pressure to 'better ourselves'—the bigger house, the better neighbourhood, the newer car, the more responsible job with more financial reward, the higher-achieving school, the more stylish clothes, the more exotic holiday and the more important friends. If we allow ourselves to fall into this trap, we will be robbed of all our peace because the love of power and possessions has an insatiable appetite that always demands more.

When we are born into the family of God, our minds are transformed by the Holy Spirit so that we can live with the 'upside-down economy' that Christ demands of us and, in doing so, find his peace. Jesus said that he gives us a peace that the world cannot give or understand, so we should not be troubled or afraid (John 14:27) to stand up and be different.

Humility is key to retaining this peace. Humility is the attitude that allows us to be fully focused on what and where God wants us to be, blissfully indifferent to material possessions and worldly position. The Christian who has learned the secret of seeking first the kingdom of God is able to trust God for the rest of her needs and those of her family.

Even in the midst of trouble, the humble [wo]man remains wholly at peace, for [s]he trusts in God, and not in the world.[3] *Spend some time asking the Lord to fill you with his peace.*

*

Trust or control?

MATTHEW 14:25–33

But when Peter looked around at the high waves, he was terrified and began to sink. 'Save me, Lord!' he shouted. Instantly Jesus reached out his hand and rescued him. 'O man of little faith,' Jesus said. 'Why did you doubt?'

This is the classic passage to consider when thinking about trusting Jesus. When we keep our eyes trustingly on him, we can walk through the storm over troubled waters. When we take our eyes off Jesus and look at the circumstances around us, we start to sink in the midst of them.

Having been sent away to school at a young age, my parents abroad and out of reach by phone, I quickly learned to depend on myself and my own resources, even in very difficult circumstances. I became the sort of person who, in Peter's situation, would have started gauging if I could make the swim to the shore rather than ask anyone for a helping hand.

When I became a Christian and got to know Jesus better, I learned to start trusting him in those 'sinking' situations, because there was no one else there to ask. However, it has been an ongoing struggle to learn to stop trying to control all the facets of my life in my own strength and trust that God is big enough and able to guide, provide and protect, just as he has promised.

Every day, we need to ask God to guide our thoughts, speech and actions, and acknowledge that we ultimately have no control over providing for our families or protecting them on those occasions when we are away from home. Life is so full of the unexpected and the uncertain that we need to know and trust that the God of all certainty is with us and is equally concerned about the big and the little worries in our lives.

May the God of hope fill you with all joy and peace as you trust in him, so that you may overflow with hope by the power of the Holy Spirit.
ROMANS 15:13 (NIV)

*

Trusting God with finances

LUKE 16:1–15

Jesus said, 'For neither you nor anyone else can serve two masters. You will hate one and show loyalty to the other, or else the other way round—you will be enthusiastic about one and despise the other. You cannot serve both God and money.'

As time goes by, I find I have to keep asking myself, 'Have I got my money or has my money got me?' How very easy it is to spend too much time wanting and worrying about how to earn that little bit more. Thinking that way takes Jesus off the throne of your heart and puts money firmly in his place. When I find myself in this situation, I have to make a point of handing my finances back to the Lord, so that he can be in control of my life again.

If we are letting God have control over our finances, we need to trust that he will 'supply all our needs from his riches in glory' (Philippians 4:19). Although this verse is talking about spiritual needs, God's provision is a biblical principle that also holds for our financial and practical needs.

Very few of us in the Western world really know what it's like to have to trust God for the very essentials of life unless we are faced with unexpected tragedy. Even so, it is quite legitimate for us to trust the Lord to provide for our needs, if not necessarily our wants, if we are actively trying to honour him in the way we allocate our income. I was just as thrilled when someone brought us one courgette from their allotment just in time to provide a vegetable for our meal, as I was when a vet's bill, threatening to cripple our finances, was covered by an unexpected cheque. To me, both were equally as precious, because God provided at exactly the right time.

> *O God, give me neither poverty nor riches! Give me just enough*
> *to satisfy my needs. For if I grow rich, I may become content*
> *without God. And if I am too poor, I may steal,*
> *and thus insult God's holy name.*
>
> PROVERBS 30:8b–9

✳

Trusting God for shelter and security

PSALM 34

I will praise the Lord no matter what happens… If you belong to the Lord, reverence him; for everyone who does this has everything he needs… The Lord is close to those whose hearts are breaking… The good man does not escape all troubles—he has them too. But the Lord helps him in each and every one.

Find a Bible and read the whole of this psalm. It is about trusting and reverencing the Lord, and knowing that he cares about us and provides for our physical and spiritual shelter and security.

It can be that our security is very much bound up in our power and possessions, or those of our spouses. These are the things we subconsciously trust and reverence. A well-paid, responsible job provides the lovely house and all the beautiful possessions with which to fill it, and the kudos of our own or our spouse's career provides us with the status we seek in the community and the church. Somehow we think that once we have obtained these things, we are impregnable to all that the world can throw at us. It is easy to forget that one redundancy notice, several outstanding mortgage repayments, an unwise investment, a sudden accident or a freak of nature can bring everything tumbling down around us.

Jesus said that the wise person builds their house upon the rock, so that when the storms come, the house remains standing (Matthew 7:25). What are we really building our lives upon—status and possessions or Christ the Rock of Ages? If we build our lives on Jesus, then when all is threatened with being swept away we can trust him to be our secure refuge and provide the basics we need to continue, rather than ending up blaming and accusing God for our misfortune.

Lord, help to me to realize that if I build the foundation of my life in you, I will have the strength to stand when circumstances threaten to sweep over me. Thank you that when we seek you, you answer, and deliver us from our fears (Psalm 34:4).

*

Trusting God with our food

MATTHEW 6:22–27

'Look at the birds! They don't worry about what to eat—they don't need to sow or reap or store up food—for your heavenly Father feeds them. And you are far more valuable to him than they are.'

When I was an impoverished student, a good meal was a rarity, so when free food was available I used to eat as much as I could. That experience left me struggling to keep overeating under control even though, in later life, I knew where the next meal was coming from. This is also why I don't like to see food wasted, and, being the mother of small children, I have found myself eating all their leftovers as well as my own meal. Eventually I knew it was time to deal with the whole business of eating habits that were out of control.

First, I had to realize the truth of today's verse: if God the Father is concerned enough to feed sparrows, then he is concerned enough to feed me and I don't need to overeat 'just in case'. Second, I had to realize that I don't need to over-face my children with food due to my own fears about not having enough to eat, and then find myself eating the leftovers. Third, I had to realize that if I am valuable to the Father, then I should treat myself with more respect and eat less and more sensibly.

Having dealt with these issues, I then discovered that I comfort-eat when I am stressed, tired, insecure, bored or angry! I've often struggled to shut the fridge door while asking the Lord what is in my heart that he needs to deal with this time.

Food can be a big issue when we are stuck at home with children, especially if we are also tackling insecurity, boredom, frustration, stress and anger. The key is learning to trust God for the food we need for our physical well-being, as well as trusting him to fill and heal the other hungry parts of our lives.

*Remember: 'The Lord... satisfies the thirsty and fills the hungry
with good things' (Psalm 107:8–9, NIV).*

*

Trusting God for our clothes

MATTHEW 6:28–34

*'And why worry about your clothes? Look at the field lilies! They don't
worry about theirs. Yet King Solomon in all his glory was not clothed
as beautifully as they. And if God cares so wonderfully for flowers that
are here today and gone tomorrow, won't he more surely care for you,
O [wo]men of little faith?'*

I have been severely tested in trusting God for my clothes this year.
Having realized that I would have no more pregnancies to hide
behind, there was no excuse not to lose the extra weight I'd gained
over the last ten years. What I hadn't bargained for was the amount
of clothes I would get through in shedding four stone and going
down five dress sizes. It was easy at first—my clothes were baggy
and elastic—but there comes a stage when even your support girdle
has nothing left to cling to. It meant a complete new wardrobe.

My heavenly Father certainly must have known my requirements,
because everything I've needed has come my way, some new, but
most second-hand. One lovely dress was printed with anemones
(lilies of the field) and at that moment I realized how wonderfully
God had provided.

When we know that we can trust the Lord to provide the
clothing we need, even for special events, we can spend our time
more beneficially allowing the Lord to make us beautiful on the
inside (1 Peter 3:3–4), cultivating a quiet and gentle spirit which is
pleasing to him.

Being beautiful inside is about allowing the Holy Spirit to produce abundant fruit in our lives (Galatians 5:22–23), so that when people meet us, they don't immediately notice what we are wearing or how our hair or make-up is fixed, but see Jesus shining through us.

*Lord, help us to remember that you care for us
and will provide for all our needs.*

*

Trusting God with our future

PSALM 139:16–17

You saw me before I was born and scheduled each day of my life before I began to breathe. Every day was recorded in your Book! How precious it is, Lord, to realize that you are thinking about me constantly!

It is actually five years since I wrote the Bible reading note that slotted in at this point in *Day by Day with God*. It was interesting to read how I saw the future back then, now that I am living in it. The verse I quoted then was one that I've tried to live by all my Christian life: 'In everything you do, put God first, and he will direct you and crown your efforts with success' (Proverbs 3:6).

What amazes me about this verse in connection with the new verse that I've quoted above is that the Lord has scheduled every day of our futures, and that our futures are precious to him. To me, this means that if we are putting him first in our lives, our efforts are sure to be crowned with his definition of success because we will be living according to his plan—his pre-ordained best for us.

Five years ago I would never have believed that what has, in fact, happened in my life since then would be possible: it wasn't even on the radar of my wildest dreams. One thing I can say, however, is that I have committed every step of the way to the Lord, not quite knowing what each step would lead to next. Sometimes the steps have been scary, but I've known the Lord directing my path. I write more about the 'how' of that in the readings on guidance (pp. 159–177). Right now I want to encourage you that nothing is impossible with God if we commit our way to him. Do that, and you will be able to look back in amazement rather than anger.

Thank you, Lord, that you know the plans you have for us, and that they are plans for a future and a hope. Help us to trust that you can indeed do more than we can ever hope or imagine (Jeremiah 29:11; Ephesians 3:20).

*

Trusting God with eternity

ROMANS 8:31–39

For I am convinced that nothing can ever separate us from his love. Death can't, and life can't. The angels won't, and all the powers of hell itself cannot keep God's love away. Our fears for today, our worries about tomorrow, or where we are—high above the sky, or in the deepest ocean—nothing will ever be able to separate us from the love of God demonstrated by our Lord Jesus Christ when he died for us.

When I had a miscarriage, I was taken into hospital. I remember coming round in the recovery room and thinking about the incredible lack of control I had experienced in losing consciousness and slipping into the nothingness of the anaesthetic. I began to wonder if this was what dying was like, and it left me feeling quite worried. I knew that there was no avoiding death—we all have to face it—but it can be a struggle to learn to trust God in the face of our uncertainties.

We can never know what death is like, or what is beyond it, until we come to that moment, so all we can do is to have faith in what God has promised in his word. Faith is 'the certainty that what we hope for is waiting for us, even though we cannot see it ahead' (Hebrews 11:1b). What we have been promised is eternal life if we believe in God's one and only Son, Jesus, who was given for us (John 3:16). The two go together hand in hand.

Jesus says that we should trust him—that he has gone ahead of us to prepare a place for us in the Father's presence (John 14:2–3). When we have learned to trust him in our earthly life and have experienced his faithfulness, trusting him for the last hurdle becomes easier.

Father God, thank you that nothing can separate us from your love—not life, and not even death—due to the precious gift you gave us in Jesus, your son.

---

1   Paul Wilson, *The Little Book of Calm* (Penguin, 1999).
2   *Why Men Don't Iron*, Channel Four (30 June 1998).
3   à Kempis, *The Imitation of Christ*, p. 70.

Living a simple life

Having looked at how we can find peace through our relationship with Jesus, I feel it would be appropriate to consider the area of life that causes me the least peace—my hectic domestic lifestyle and managing an abundance of possessions—and what I have tried to do, in the words of the prophet Jeremiah, to bring 'peace where there is no peace' (Jeremiah 6:14).

I wrote the following article in 1999, well before the current fashion for television programmes telling us how to de-junk our homes and simplify our lives. It seems to me these programmes reflect the heart cry of people whose lives are spiralling out of control and who are looking for inner peace—but in all the wrong places. It is unfortunate that our politically correct culture cannot advocate, on prime-time TV, a good bout of confession, absolution and prayer ministry combined with a practical de-junk, to get to the root of the problem! When I hear the presenter say, 'That's right. Just let the tears out...' I want to add a prayer in Jesus' name that the poor person will find lasting wholeness and healing, and the new purpose and direction that only Jesus can give. Anyway, this is how I learned to live a simple life.

*

Jesus said, 'Come to me and I will give you rest—all of you who work so hard beneath a heavy yoke. Wear my yoke—for it fits perfectly—and let me teach you; for I am gentle and humble, and you shall find rest for your souls; for I give you only light burdens.'
MATTHEW 11:28–30

I have often wondered if I am under some sort of unacknowledged curse because I am 'Saturday's child' and, according to the English childhood rhyme, I have to 'work hard for my living'. Even when I accidentally broke the christening mug with the offending statement on it, life became no less hectic and the burdens no less!

To be honest, I am sure it is nothing to do with the day I was born, but that my hectic schedule and material burdens are factors of contemporary living. We are all becoming busier, and the demands made upon us have become so great that even advances in technology cannot effectively ease the burden. The fact that we often live in isolation from each other, even within the immediate family, also means that there may be nobody around to share the burden of necessary labour.

The only person who can take this burden off our shoulders is Jesus. When we come to know Jesus as our personal friend and saviour, the priorities in our life begin to change. If we are keeping our eyes fixed on him, suddenly the desire to accumulate possessions, the drive to succeed at work at all costs, the pressure to look as fantastic as a supermodel and to live the life of the rich and famous all take a back seat. All that matters is that we are living according to the Father's plan for our life and seeking to bless our family, friends, colleagues and neighbours by serving them as if they were Christ himself (Matthew 6:33).

When life is boiled down to the basic level of 'seeking first the kingdom of God', it becomes truly 'simple' (that is, uncluttered) and 'easy' (in other words, lacking in stress). The spiritual notion of 'simplicity' contains the connotation of 'easiness', because it demands that everything unnecessary be stripped away. Spiritual or inner simplicity is basically the freedom in our hearts and minds from uncontrolled desires. It allows us to seek nothing but the will of God and the good of others. It is the spiritual detachment from earthly things that allows us to appreciate the world around us without feeling that we have to control or possess the desired person or object.

If the multiplicity of things that distract us from seeking God are removed, then life will become more focused and easier. The writer of Hebrews (12:1) encourages us to strip off all that holds us back from running the race that God has set before us. If we do this, the fruit of our obedience is to know the peace that the world cannot give but that so many of us desire (John 14:27).

Many people think that to live with this level of simplicity is impossible unless you take monastic vows and retreat from the world. In actual fact, simplicity can be achieved in secular life with a little examining of one's lifestyle and by making a few appropriate adjustments. This decision often means that we are called to swim against the flow of worldly expectations, and that can be difficult. None of us likes being criticized by our friends: we want to be accepted. Jesus did warn us, however, that we will attract criticism if we follow him (John 15:20).

So how can we start to make our lives simple in the true sense of the word? Outer simplicity is, by necessity, the reflection of inner simplicity, and this is where the de-junking programmes on TV stumble: they deal mainly with symptoms. They sometimes attempt to get at the root of the problem, but a good cry and throwing something reminding you of a past hurt into a crushing machine isn't always going to produce total inner healing. Inner simplicity means having your heart and mind de-junked: there must be an inner commitment to let God have his way in your inner life, or outward simplicity will only be the fruit of legalism—and that's hard work.

Our lives speak out of the abundance of our hearts (Mark 7:21), so true inner simplicity and wholeness will be reflected in the way we organize our schedules and our living environments. This could be equated to the monastic vow of 'poverty', the vow that has a bearing on the relationship with material things, and human acquisitiveness. 'Chastity' has to do with relationships with others, and 'obedience' with the relationship with God. Getting to grips with 'poverty' will naturally lead the disciple to explore the other two, but we'll leave that for another time...

For me, the initial search for spiritual simplicity began with a quiet prayer asking to be free of the tendency to desire and hang on to all the earthly extras that clutter up my life and stop me focusing on Jesus:

O Lord, give me neither poverty nor riches, but give me only my daily bread. Otherwise, I may have too much and disown you and say, 'Who is the Lord?' Or I may become poor and steal, and so dishonour the name of my God.

PROVERBS 30:7–9 (NIV)

I really wanted to know the secret of being 'content in any and every situation, whether well fed or hungry, whether living in plenty or in want' (Philippians 4:12b, NIV).

The material things we may need to let the Lord speak to us about could include money, work, security, clothes, food and entertainment. Let's have a whistle-stop tour, and then you can take an in-depth look at each area in your own and the Lord's time. It took me several years to peel away the excesses in various areas of my life—not helped by the fact that car boot sales are always on Sundays, and I can't bring myself to take my junk to one on the Sabbath!

Money: Jesus had more to say about money than any other issue. He said that we cannot serve God and money—we will hate one and love the other (Matthew 6:24). We must develop the attitude that all our wealth belongs to the Lord. I find that it helps to give a set proportion of our income to the work of God's kingdom through the church. Once we honour that commitment, God seems to stretch what is left to cover our needs and some of our wants (Proverbs 3:9–10).

Home: As a clergy couple living in tied accommodation, we sometimes worry that we have nowhere to call our own. We have to keep reminding ourselves that Jesus said, 'Foxes have holes and birds of the air have nests, but the Son of Man has no place to lay his head' (Matthew 8:20, NIV) and that 'a servant is not above his master' (Matthew 10:24), so we shouldn't expect too much! Our security has to be in the Lord, not four walls and a tiled roof. If we are not attached to a place, we have the freedom to leave it when he calls us on.

Possessions: Home is not just the structure of a house, but its contents. An uncluttered heart will have an uncluttered home. If we have no clutter to be dusting and tidying all day, we are free to spend our time on tasks that are more beneficial to the kingdom of God. Stock-take and dispose of unnecessary stuff constructively, because 'a man's [or woman's] life does not consist in the abundance of his [her] possessions' (Luke 12:15, NIV).

Work: We must understand that it is not our work that gives us what we have; it is the grace of God. When we truly grasp that, we become free to ask whether we should be occupied in the job that we are doing. Is it really what God wants us to do or are we doing it for the money, the prestige, to find personal significance or to exert power over others? Maybe we need to change our attitude, or maybe we need to change our job.

Clothes: This is a dangerous subject to mention to a readership of women! Jesus said that we should not worry about what we wear: not even King Solomon was dressed as beautifully as the lilies of the field (Matthew 6:28–34). All of us have too many clothes in our wardrobes—things that are the wrong size, the wrong colour, an inappropriate style and kept 'just in case'. Look at your lifestyle, assess your real needs, find out which colours and lines really suit you and then discard (preferably, recycle) anything that doesn't fall into these categories. The 'what-to-wear' factor will decrease significantly and then disappear.

Food, its supply and preparation: Food is a cult these days: one look at women's magazines demonstrates this. Menus have become more complex and elaborate, and ingredients have become more exotic and harder to find. The consequence of following this trend is excess expenditure of time and money. Food does not have to be fancy to be good for you! Find out your basic daily food requirements and reassess your diet and shopping list. I am sure I could cut my list by a third without even trying. Then a treat becomes just that—a treat—and not a right (unless it's chocolate, of course!).

It would be impossible to give an adequate treatment of all the aspects of living a simple life in such a short chapter. If reading this has whetted your appetite to find out more, there are some books recommended below. The main point to remember, though, is that our outward lifestyle should be a reflection of our inner desire to put Jesus first. Outward simplicity in isolation from this principle should not become our god!

FURTHER READING

Keep it Simple: Creating Your Own Rule for Life, Nick Page (HarperCollins, 1999)

The Way of Holiness, Robert Van de Weyer (Fount, 1992)

A Celebration of Discipline, Richard Foster (Hodder and Stoughton, 1989)

Money, Sex and Power, Richard Foster (Hodder and Stoughton, 1985

Freedom of Simplicity, Richard Foster (Triangle/SPCK, 1981)

Compassion and mercy

Get rid of all bitterness, rage and anger, brawling and slander, along with every form of malice. Be kind and compassionate to one another, forgiving each other, just as in Christ God forgave you.
EPHESIANS 4:31–32 (NIV)

I shared with you at the very start of this book that these verses were crucial in leading me to a place where God could break into my life, touch me, heal me and change me. It is therefore no coincidence that developing compassion and kindness, or, in the case of the following Bible reading notes, its close relative mercy, has been an important marker in helping to direct my journey from the wilderness into my personal promised land.

Compassion and mercy are the opposite attributes to the bitterness and anger that used to fill my life, and that's why I want these attributes to be found in my present life, rather than those old ones. When the Lord begins to pervade your being with his presence, which is developed by cultivating inner solitude and peace, compassion and mercy have all the sustenance they need to grow. If you have learnt how to forgive others from the heart, then compassion and mercy will not be far behind, and what is wonderful about these attributes is that they are not just fuzzy feelings that we keep to ourselves, but attributes that are revealed in our actions. Are you ready for action?

*

God's compassion and mercy

He is merciful and tender [compassionate] towards those who don't deserve it; he is slow to get angry and full of kindness and love. He never bears a grudge, nor remains angry forever. He has not punished us as we deserve for our sins, for his mercy towards those who fear and honour him is as great as the height of the heavens above the earth.

'Compassion' and 'mercy' are not words we tend to think about much these days. We think more in terms of 'love', a word that has had its innate dynamic power replaced by sentimentality and inaction. Compassion and mercy are active expressions of love for others that reflect the nature of God in whose image we are created. We often forget that God is merciful and compassionate; he can seem too big and far away to have characteristics like that!

Mercy actually means to have forbearance (patience) and a forgiving disposition towards someone who is in your power. Compassion means to have fellow feeling for the suffering and sorrow of others, and to have pity on the unfortunate.

When we enter a living relationship with God the Father through Jesus Christ, we get to know and understand that God is merciful towards us. God is not like humans: he does not have to prove his power by being unyielding towards us. He has a forgiving disposition and is waiting patiently to help us in the difficult times we experience. He does not condemn us for our struggles, failure and difficulties. He feels for us in them—he is ultimately compassionate.

Lord, we often forget that you are merciful, that you deal with us patiently—always ready to forgive. Renew in us a fresh understanding of your nature so that we are not hesitant about coming to you with our difficulties. Thank you that you feel for us in the sorrows we experience. You are not distant from us; you have entered into our daily struggles. Help us to acknowledge your presence with us today and every day.

*

God's compassion and faithfulness

LAMENTATIONS 3:15–33

Yet there is one ray of hope: his compassion never ends. It is only the Lord's mercies that have kept us from complete destruction. Great is his faithfulness; his lovingkindness begins afresh every day...

The Lord will not abandon [a man] forever. Although God gives him grief, yet he will show compassion too, according to the greatness of his lovingkindness. For he does not enjoy afflicting men and causing sorrow.

This passage describes the feelings of someone who has had many years of suffering, experiencing grief that has brought them close to utter despair. However, this person is ready to acknowledge that the only ray of hope in their dire situation is the unending compassion of the Lord.

The Lord's compassion for us doesn't mean that he is always going to allow life to treat us kindly. We live in a world in which we will have sorrow and difficulties to face. We need to hold on to the knowledge that God is 'wonderfully good to those who wait for him' (Lamentations 3:25). The Lord doesn't enjoy our affliction; he is compassionate and will show it. The things we suffer teach us a lot about ourselves and about the Lord. We need to make time to look back, listen and learn what it is he is trying to show us.

Verses 31–33 (the second paragraph in the passage quoted

above) were recently on my desk calendar. Printed below them was the comment, 'The years teach us much that the days know little about.' When we are young in our faith, this can be hard to understand, because we haven't travelled very far in our walk with Jesus. As we continue to follow Jesus and the road stretches out behind us, we can see that, despite the difficult times, the Lord has been faithful and the years we have followed him have taught us much that is invisible from day to day.

> *Take some time to think back over your Christian life. Remember the events that brought you to faith and the milestones that you have passed along the way. Spend time thanking the Lord for his compassion and faithfulness, especially in the situations that seemed hard to bear at the time, but that have produced fruit in your life in the long term. If you can't remember, it may be worth thinking about keeping a journal.*

*

The compassionate father

LUKE 15:11–24

So he returned home to his father. And while he was still a long distance away, his father saw him coming, and was filled with loving pity [compassion] and ran and embraced him and kissed him… The father said… 'We must celebrate with a feast. For this son of mine was dead and has returned to life. He was lost and is found.'

Our understanding of Jesus' and thus the Father's compassion for the lost is well illustrated in the parable of the prodigal son. The younger son has demanded his inheritance in advance, sold it and squandered the money far away from home, becoming destitute.

Eventually his circumstances become so bad that the son decides that life at home as a slave will be better than the condition he has been reduced to. In a miraculous act of submission and humility, he returns home.

The attitude of the father is the more amazing aspect of this story. In the first place, most human fathers would have refused to give the son his inheritance in advance. If a son sells his part of the family farm, it usually leads to division, anger and bitterness on the part of the rejected father. This son goes one step further and squanders the money rather than re-investing it. Everything the father worked for and the son was given is gone. Most human fathers would have disowned the negligent son by now, but not the father in the story.

This father has never given up having compassion for his son; his love is unconditional. The father is certainly hurt, rejected and disappointed, but never gives up hope that his son will come home again, and is constantly watching out for him.

This is Jesus' picture of God the Father, whom we have rejected and disappointed but whose compassion for his lost children is unending. He is constantly looking out for any sign that we may be heading back home into relationship with him.

Father God, thank you for your unconditional love. May I never be hesitant in running back to you, however much I think I may have squandered what you have given me.

Jesus' humanity and compassion

HEBREWS 2:8B–18

And it was necessary for Jesus to be like us, his brothers, so that he could be our merciful and faithful high priest before God… For since he himself has now been through suffering and temptation, he knows what it is like when we suffer and are tempted, and he is wonderfully able to help us.

We have thought a little bit about God's mercy and compassion towards us, but how can we be sure that he really knows what it is like to experience the things we experience?

God the Father loves humankind with an unfathomable love and, to demonstrate that to us in a way that we could understand, he sent Jesus, his son, to earth to live among us and experience the daily trials and temptations that we face. That is how we can be sure that our situation is made intimately clear to God the Father in heaven, because Jesus, who mediates and pleads for us, has suffered in human form and had fellow feeling for our situation.

Jesus knows what it is like to be homeless and outcast, a refugee chased from his homeland to live in an alien culture, to go in fear of his life, to bear the stigma of illegitimacy, to lack possessions and be hungry, to be tempted, and to lose a loved one. He experienced torture, misrepresentation and betrayal. He was falsely accused, branded a criminal and executed unjustly. The Bible tells us that he bore our sorrows and was acquainted with the bitterest grief (Isaiah 53:3). Nothing that any of us has experienced can be equated with that.

In addition, Jesus took the burden of the sin of the world on his shoulders when he died on the cross and experienced being forsaken by God. He is therefore intimately acquainted with our human condition and wonderfully able to help us when we call upon him.

Lord Jesus, when I find myself feeling that no one understands what I am going through, remind me that you know what I am suffering because you have walked the same path, and so you are wonderfully able to help me.

Jesus sheds tears of compassion

JOHN 11:11–45

When Mary arrived where Jesus was, she fell down at his feet, saying, 'Sir, if you had been here, my brother would still be alive.' When Jesus saw her weeping and the Jewish leaders wailing with her, he was moved with indignation and deeply troubled. 'Where is he buried?' he asked them. They told him, 'Come and see.' Tears came to Jesus' eyes.

When Jesus heard that his friend Lazarus had died, he travelled to the place where he was buried and met Mary, Lazarus' sister. She was consumed with grief and probably indignation that Jesus had not arrived sooner. Jesus looked at the gathering; he saw Mary's grief and the professional wailing of the mourners and was moved with a compassion that welled up into indignation (v. 33) and (in the original Greek) anger (v. 38).

Jesus was not angry with himself for being late, or with Mary for her emotions or the mourners for their lack of genuine compassion. He identified with Mary's grief because he too had loved Lazarus, but he was indignant at the power that death held over people because sin had cut them off from the Father. Jesus' tears were more for the plight of humanity than for his friend Lazarus.

We know that Jesus felt a deep sense of compassion in this situation because the verb used for Jesus' weeping is a different verb, with more intense feeling, than the one used to describe Mary's grief or the grief of the other mourners. His compassion and indignation did not remain merely an emotion. Jesus used this opportunity to raise Lazarus from the dead, demonstrating that he, Jesus, had power over death—because he would eventually show himself to be the Resurrection and the Life.

Lord, thank you that your love for us is so strong that you feel anger at the power that sin and death hold over us. Thank you, Lord, that your resurrection power is stronger than death. Give us the same indignation that you felt, so that by the power of your Holy Spirit we may constantly seek to bring people into your saving presence. Amen

∗

Jesus shows compassion for the lost

MATTHEW 9:35—10:10

Wherever [Jesus] went he healed people of every sort of illness. And what pity [compassion] he felt for the crowds that came, because their problems were so great and they didn't know what to do or where to go for help. They were like sheep without a shepherd... Jesus called his twelve disciples to him, and gave them authority to cast out evil spirits and to heal every kind of sickness and disease.

If we want to know what God is really like, we need to look at Jesus—his person, life and work—because 'Christ is the exact likeness of the unseen God' (Colossians 1:15). Jesus didn't become a man just so that God could prove he understood our plight by going through the same problems as us, but so that we could see what God is really like—a compassionate and merciful Father.

In the passage above, we see Jesus' reaction to the thronging crowds that flocked to see him and listen to him. He could see their innermost needs and their desperation and he felt compassion for them because they were lost, without anyone to guide and protect them. It would be easy to think that this compassion was a 'pretty little feeling' that Jesus had, but the Greek word used here means that it 'got him in the guts'. Jesus didn't think, 'Oh, the poor little lost souls!' He was wracked to his innermost being over the plight of people who had fallen out of relationship with their creator to the extent that they did not know where to turn.

Jesus didn't allow compassion to stop with feelings; he *did* something. He told the disciples to pray for more workers to spread the good news and then he chose twelve of them, filled them with the power of his Spirit and sent them out to preach and heal.

We learn from this passage the depth of God's compassion for us and that he is a God of action.

Lord, give me a greater depth of understanding and compassion
for the lost people in my family and community. Give me a burden
to pray for them and a willingness to put into action what you lay
on my heart. Amen

*

Jesus shows compassion for outcasts

MARK 1:38–45

Once a leper came and knelt in front of [Jesus] and begged to be healed.
'If you want to, you can make me well again,' he pleaded. Jesus, moved
with pity [compassion], touched him and said, 'I want to. Be healed!'

Jesus also shows us by his example that God the Father is touched to the core by the outcasts of society. Here we see Jesus being moved with compassion for a leper. In those days, leprosy was considered a terrible disease. Even today, left untreated, it destroys the nerves under the skin, leading to paralysis and injuries of the hands, feet and face. In biblical times, those who developed leprosy were made to live in isolation, not welcomed among the healthy and whole members of the community.

In today's Western society we don't meet lepers, but our culture has created contemporary versions of the leper—all sorts of people with whom we would rather not associate. We could mention the mentally ill, the physically disabled, the homeless and the emotionally needy. Some people would rather not be associated with anyone who doesn't match up to their idea of 'the beautiful set' and are prejudiced against age, skin colour, size and religious belief.

The leper in the story was crying out, 'Lord, make me well... I want to be included, I want to be loved and accepted! You can do it if you want to!' Jesus says, 'I want to! Be healed!' Apart from the challenge of believing that Jesus can still heal today, the challenge for us is whether or not we allow ourselves to be moved with the same compassion for today's social outcasts as Jesus was towards that leper. Are we willing to say to the Lord, 'I want to!' We needn't look much further than the next church pew or the corner of the coffee lounge for the outcast and the rejected.

Lord, open our eyes to see the outcasts in our midst. Give us the courage to overcome our prejudices and show acts of mercy towards those who feel left out and rejected. Give us your love, wisdom and guidance in every situation. Amen

*

Jesus shows compassion for the sick

MATTHEW 20:29–34

Two blind men were sitting beside the road and when they heard that Jesus was coming that way, they began shouting, 'Sir, King David's Son, have mercy on us!' ... Jesus called, 'What do you want me to do for you?' 'Sir,' they said, 'we want to be able to see!' Jesus was moved with pity for them and touched their eyes. And instantly they could see, and followed him.

In the Gospels we read about Jesus' compassion for the sick and how he healed people. What is interesting about this story is that the blind men shouted, 'Have mercy upon us!' They knew that Jesus had power to heal them: they were at his mercy.

Jesus knew exactly what the blind men wanted him to do for them, yet he asked them, 'What do you want me to do for you?' Jesus wanted to hear with his own ears what they thought he could grant them. 'We want to see!' they shouted. Jesus, moved with compassion, had mercy on them and touched their eyes. They were healed and followed him.

Recently a friend told me that she felt the Lord had a question for me: 'What do you want me to do for you?' At first I couldn't answer, I didn't think there was anything that I wanted God to do for me. Eventually I realized that I had lost sight of the fact that Jesus had the compassion and the mercy (power) to do even the simplest thing that, in my need, I asked for. We can all be like blind people sitting at the edge of the road. When Jesus comes by, we are convinced that either our need or God's power is not great enough. We sit there, not daring to raise our voices.

Jesus has compassion on the physically, spiritually, emotionally and mentally sick. We need to regain the realization that he has not only the compassion but also the mercy and power to heal.

*Jesus is speaking to you. He is asking, 'What can I do for you?'
How will you answer that question?*

*

Jesus shows compassion for the needy

MARK 8:1–9

One day about this time as another great crowd gathered, the people ran out of food again. Jesus called his disciples to discuss the situation.

'I pity these people,' he said, 'for they have been here three days, and have nothing left to eat. And if I send them home without feeding them, they will faint along the road! For some of them have come a long distance.'

Jesus had already miraculously fed one large crowd that had come out for the day without any food (Mark 6:35–45). Perhaps they had thought they wouldn't be there long and would be home in time for tea. However, the people had been so attentive to Jesus that, before they knew it, they were hungry. Then Jesus multiplied five loaves and two fish to feed five thousand men.

Next time the crowds had come prepared. They had listened to Jesus for three days, but *now* they had run out of food. Jesus felt compassion for them. He could see that they had been so keen to hear the truth of the kingdom that they had stayed longer than their food had lasted. Some of them had travelled a long way to listen to Jesus. He knew that they would faint along the road home.

Initially Jesus had been concerned because the crowd was spiritually lost. He now had compassion on them because, in their desire to seek, they had forgotten their practical needs. Jesus has compassion for both our spiritual and our physical needs.

We must also learn to feel compassion for the needy and put it into action with acts of mercy. It is right to call 'helping the needy' an 'act of mercy', because in the affluent West we have the power to do something about the needs of the poor and the obligation to use that power for others' benefit.

Read Matthew 25:34–46. Think about practical acts of mercy you can do in your community and further afield.

*

Jesus shows compassion for children

MARK 10:13–16

Once when some mothers were bringing their children to Jesus to bless them, the disciples shooed them away, telling them not to bother him. But when Jesus saw what was happening he was very displeased with his disciples and said to them, 'Let the children come to me, for the Kingdom of God belongs to such as they. Don't send them away! ...' Then he took the children into his arms and placed his hands on their heads and he blessed them.

Many of us have been brought up with the belief that 'children should be seen and not heard'. Many people feel that it's better if children are not seen at all: what the adults are doing is too important to be interrupted by demanding children.

Women and children were among the least important in the society of Jesus' time. The disciples were sure that they shouldn't bother Jesus. But Jesus has a habit of up-ending all our social pre-conceptions, and he tells the disciples to let the children come to him.

Many times I have seen mothers with small children standing in the cold outside a church because there was nowhere else to go to escape the grimaces of the congregation. What must this say to these mothers, many who have come to church for the first time for a wedding or a christening?

If you have small children, there should be no need for you to apologize for them. Challenge your church to be more constructive! Those of us whose children are now older need to remind ourselves how it felt, and be compassionate, helping others in the ways we would have liked to have been helped, or were helped. Compassionate acts of mercy give small children and their mothers a positive meeting with Jesus that can only affect their lives for the better.

Lord, give me compassion for small children and their mothers.
Help me to remember that you welcomed and blessed children.
Give me the grace to offer help to those who are struggling. Make
our churches loving and welcoming. Amen

*

Jesus shows compassion for the moment

LUKE 8:40–56

A messenger arrived from Jairus' home with the news that the little girl
was dead. 'She's gone... there's no use troubling the Teacher now.' But
when Jesus heard what had happened, he said to the father, 'Don't be
afraid! Just trust me, and she'll be all right.' ... Then he took her by the
hand and called, 'Get up, little girl!' And at that moment her life
returned and she jumped up. 'Give her something to eat!' he said. Her
parents were overcome with happiness.

I am one of those women who constantly struggle to balance being
a 'Mary' or a 'Martha', spending time with Jesus or doing what
needs to be done. The 'Mary' attitude has been so exalted that we
can get quite depressed if we feel that our whole life is full of
cleaning and cooking!

What I love about this passage is how Jesus juxtaposes the kingdom of God and practical needs in almost one breath. First he raises
Jairus' daughter from the dead and then tells her parents to feed her!
We don't know how long the little girl had been ill, but she was
probably very weak and dehydrated. Jesus knew it was important
that the girl's physical needs were met: it was not appropriate for
her to sit prettily on her bed while he used the opportunity to teach
the people.

It is good for us to learn that Jesus was not afraid to do what was appropriate for the particular moment, whether the act was of supreme spiritual significance or a small physical act of service in private. It can be as important to offer people a cup of tea as to offer them prayer. Preferably they should be offered both, in the order that fits the situation!

The compassionate and merciful heart listens to what God the Father is saying in a situation and acts accordingly. We have no need constantly to perform the spectacular to impress God or others. The Lord looks on the heart, and our deeds are a reflection of its content.

Lord, keep me from 'performance ministry'. Help me always to see with your eyes and act with your love. Amen

*

The business of compassion

ZECHARIAH 7:8–9

Then this message from the Lord came to Zechariah. 'Tell them to be honest and fair—and not to take bribes—and to be merciful and kind to everyone. Tell them to stop oppressing widows and orphans, foreigners and poor people, and to stop plotting evil against each other.'

We have looked at the compassionate and merciful nature of God and how it is revealed through Jesus, giving us many examples that we can apply in our personal life and in how we relate to others. We have seen that compassion is not just a 'gooey' feeling that we get when we feel 'sort of sorry' for someone, but it is a deep gut reaction, often born of our ability to identify with the sufferer through our own experience. We have seen that compassion is not just the ability to empathize but to take positive action.

Like many aspects of the Christian life, compassion is not an optional extra; it is a command—an extension of the command to love our neighbour as ourselves. Obeying a command is a conscious decision of the will; it is not a matter of waiting to be moved by emotion or the Holy Spirit, although he does empower us to carry the decision through.

The passage above makes us look at taking compassion into the marketplace, the workplace and the corridors of power—cold, calculating places. Those of us who move in such circles are often called upon to be tough, but the Lord calls us to be compassionate and merciful, and equates that with being honest and fair. It is very easy to take advantage of the powerless in society, but we have a God who commands that we see they get a fair deal.

Lord, help me today in the difficult decisions I have to take, when showing your compassion may fly in the face of what is considered clever and to be expected in our secular society. Help me to be ready to give a good account about what I have decided. Amen

*

Passing on help and comfort

2 CORINTHIANS 1:3–11

When others are troubled, needing our sympathy and encouragement, we can pass on to them this same help and comfort God has given us. You can be sure that the more we undergo sufferings for Christ, the more he will shower us with his comfort and encouragement.

When my husband was training for the ministry, I belonged to a group of students' wives who met for prayer, study and encouragement. I remember a meeting when everyone was very excited because one of the wives was saying that the Lord had healed her of post-natal depression. I remember thinking, 'Big deal! What's that, anyway?' I was very young and had had no children myself, so I didn't understand why there was so much rejoicing. I had no understanding or compassion, no 'fellow feeling', because the situation was beyond my experience.

Eight years later, I *was* that woman. As I explained at the beginning of this book, I had had three babies in quick succession and a bad depression after the first two, which was undiagnosed and thus untreated. Eventually I was confronted by my situation. The Lord opened 'a window of opportunity' and I opened myself to the possibility that he could change me: I wanted to be healed and whole. I was prayed for by two lovely women counsellors and instantly healed. Although I still had much to learn, people could testify to the fact that I was changed.

As a result of this experience, I can now enter into the world of those who suffer in the same way. I have a frame of reference for 'fellow feeling'—a compassion that wasn't there before.

When we have experienced particular difficulties, we should be better equipped as a result to help others who are going through similar problems. Our experience should enable us to show them understanding and Jesus' compassion by putting his love into action.

What difficult things have you experienced? Ask the Lord to help you come to terms with these things enough to be able to show compassion and offer help to others in the same circumstances.

*

Compassion, forgiveness and blessing

1 PETER 3:8–15

And now this word to all of you: You should be like one big happy family, full of sympathy towards each other, loving one another with tender hearts and humble minds. Don't repay evil for evil. Don't snap back at those who say unkind things about you. Instead, pray for God's help for them, for we are to be kind to others, and God will bless us for it.

It is strange how people use the expression 'big happy family'. Often, big families can be very unhappy because there is tension, no privacy, not enough individual attention when needed, restrictions, responsibility and resentment.

Domestic families and church families experience this when individuals (adults and children!) allow themselves to become so self-orientated that the rest of the family begins to suffer. We occasionally have to 'read the riot act' to our family because sympathy, compassion, tenderness and humility have been chased out by unkind words, selfishness, retaliation and lack of consideration for others.

If we make time to stop and ask ourselves why someone is behaving the way they are, the Lord will show us the root of the problem and give us the compassion we need to sympathize with that person, to forgive them and live patiently with them. More often than not, Jesus challenges *us* to be changed, so that we can be a channel for growth. This leads to a more encouraging attitude in us that will help the other person change too. We mustn't wait for other people to make the first move: the Lord challenges each one of us to be the compassionate peacemaker. And, as always with God, our obedience brings a blessing to all concerned.

Lord Jesus, thank you for the challenge to be compassionate.
Help us to identify and root out the attitudes we have that are not
compatible with living for you. Forgive us, and help us to be
forgiving, so that we might be a channel of blessing to others.
Amen

The compassionate parent

Therefore, as God's chosen people, holy and dearly beloved, clothe your-selves with compassion, kindness, humility, gentleness and patience. Bear with each other and forgive whatever grievances you may have against one another.
COLOSSIANS 3:12–13a (NIV)

I finished the last series of Bible readings on compassion with the verses from 1 Peter 3 about being one big happy family—not snapping back but being kind to those who hurt or offend us. Those verses were originally written to a church fellowship, but could just as easily have been written to my family and me. I was very good at snapping back and holding grievances before the Lord sorted me out. I am not saying I became a reformed character overnight—it took quite a while to re-educate my bad habits—but when you have forgiven those who have hurt you (whether they know they've hurt you or not), compassion, kindness, humility, gentleness and patience are the sort of fruit you are looking to cultivate in your life, rather than the sarcasm and angry retorts that come from a bitter heart.

This can take a fair amount of thinking through and working out in your own context. The following article was the result of my efforts to try to bring the compassion of Christ into my family of three demanding children while I was expecting my fourth. Apparently it only takes six weeks of persistence to break an old habit and create a new one, and from my experience I tend to agree!

*

I have noticed a trend in today's society to put an emphasis on child-centred parenting. It is a trap that parents can be very easily lured into because we all want the best for our children and desperately want to avoid making the same mistakes as the parents of previous generations. Parenting was once very parent-centred: the child was managed around what suited the parent; if children were seen, they were not heard; and middle-class children especially were marshalled around a very structured daily nursery regime. In an effort to compensate for this outdated practice, children now run their parents round in circles rather than vice versa.

As Christians it could be easy for us to adopt the child-centred line of thought, because it suggests the giving of selfless love by the parent who wants to show that they have understanding and compassion for the child's point of view. Letting the child rule the roost, however, is not truly loving or compassionate. A child that always gets its own way will never grow up to learn the concern for others and self-discipline that the parents are trying to instil in it by their own sacrificial example: human nature is far too self-seeking for that.

I believe that true compassion can work only within a framework of boundaries and discipline that benefits both parents and children. The Lord's kindness and compassion operate within his boundaries of justice and authority, and the same sort of balance is essential for earthly parents. I found out how this might work for parents and children during my exploratory reading into the 'how' of cloistered life. The Rule of St Benedict provided a strange but interesting place to learn about compassion within a framework of discipline: changing a few pronouns, the following advice to monks could easily have been written for mothers.

With all compassion [she] is to have care for the sick, the children, the guests and the poor, knowing for certain that in the day of judgment [s]he will have to render an account of [her] treatment of them all.[1]

I also found the Rule very liberating in the question of how to respond to children demanding snacks five minutes before tea-time.

Whatever has to be asked for or given should be asked for or given at suitable times, so that no one should be upset or saddened in the household of God… And if [she] has nothing material to give, [she] should at least offer a kind word of reply.[2]

The child-centred parent finds permission here to say 'No' kindly and gently—and without feeling guilty—if it's too close to the next meal-time to snack, or if the snacks have run out. There is no need to give in to pleas and tantrums just for a minute's peace. That is what I used to do during my depression—I couldn't bear the noise and stress—but giving in did neither the children nor me any good. It only reinforced bad habits, and made me cross when they wouldn't eat their meal. My own fault, of course!

We all know the problems of serving something that everyone likes to eat. The Rule gave me a way to cook with compassion, or perhaps I should call it 'culinary flexibility within limits'. Listen to this:

Allow for the weaknesses of different eaters; so that if some cannot eat of the one dish [they] may still make a meal of the other.[3]

It isn't kind and compassionate to make someone sit for hours staring at food they're not going to eat. They'll become resentful and you'll get cross. Would you eat cold congealed beef gristle? I wouldn't. Past generations of my family have been subjected to that treatment, but I decided to treat the next generation differently. Since then, I have tried to ensure that there is some choice at meal-times, finance permitting.

It is, however, a different situation when a child rejects something they like, out of pure awkwardness. I used to get so embroiled in these meal-time rows that occasionally I'd throw the food across the room to save the children doing it! (No, that is not an excuse for you to do the same!) Now I prefer the following advice:

If something is offered… and he rejects it, then when he does want what he previously rejected, or something else, he is not to receive anything at all until he makes suitable satisfaction.[4]

Can you believe that monks could behave so much like two-year-olds as to need that advice? I find it encouraging. Monks and toddlers alike are advised to quieten down, sit at the table and say 'sorry'. Wonderful!

It is so important in all this to remember the 'kind word of reply' mentioned above. I physically wince when I hear mothers scolding their toddlers loudly in supermarkets—mainly because I've been there, done that and regret it bitterly, but also because it could be done firmly but quietly and kindly. It is one thing not wanting to berate a small child in that manner, but it is quite another for a stressed-out, exhausted mum to be able to break out of the vicious circle and speak to her child with kindness and compassion. It can be done, though, if you let the Lord change you on the inside.

Susan Haydon-Knowell has commented that 'we communicate to our children what we really are'.[5] Before God changed my heart, all I was communicating was frustration and resentment, because that is how I perceived my situation. The children picked up these attitudes and simply behaved like a mirror. If there was no kindness and compassion in me because of what I was like inside, why was I so shocked to see the same attitudes appearing in them?

Despite inward change, old habits die hard. Sometimes we need conscious discipline to help us unlearn the negative and allow new fruit room to grow. Susan Haydon-Knowell suggests being 'as polite to your children as you would be to a guest in your own home… if you shout, nag or ignore them, they will behave in the same way towards each other'.[6] This practice can initially seem artificial, but it soon becomes natural if it comes from a compassionate heart. If you stick at it, it can only take six weeks to establish a new pattern of behaviour.

It may seem strange to you that I have had to delve into the writings of a monk from the sixth century to find authoritative anchor points for my life, but I firmly belief that if we are seeking to work out our salvation with fear and trembling (Philippians 2:12), the Lord provides the right means to meet us in our particular need, even if he has to reach out through four hundred years of history.

Anyway, I do hope it has helped you—and next time you lift a plate in frustration to slam baked beans against the wall, think compassion; think St Benedict!

P.S. Now I have teenagers, maybe I should investigate the following: 'No one should be so bold as to take any food or drink before or after the regular meal time.'[7] Or maybe that is advice for combating middle-age spread!

This is a major revision of the article 'The Compassionate Parent' which appeared in *Renewal* 226, March 1995, pages 30–31. Used with permission.

1   *The Rule*, 31:9.
2   *The Rule*, 31:18–19 and 31:13.
3   *The Rule*, 39:1b–2.
4   *The Rule*, 43:19.
5   S. Haydon-Knowell, *How to be a Better Leader's Wife* (Coastlands, 1983), p. 12.
6   Haydon-Knowell, *How to be a Better Leader's Wife*, p. 13.
7   *The Rule*, 43:18.

Some thoughts on prayer

So far, we've spent quite a while looking at how we can live in God's presence, find his peace and fill our hearts with his loving compassion and mercy. These studies reflected my early experiences of trying to find God in my spiritual desert. After a while, I began to realize that if I didn't find some kind of undergirding framework for my journey, I could find myself with a very nebulous sort of spirituality, when I really wanted to regain what I knew and had experienced as a new Christian long before I'd had children.

Looking back, I can see that I wrote the following set of Bible readings on prayer at this transition point. Practising the presence of God had helped me to rediscover my relationship with God in difficult times, but now I wanted to work my way back to an experience of faith that would stand me in good stead when the desert years were over. The first six of these readings on prayer are more representative of my early struggles: they are quite subjective and experimental. In the final eight readings I can almost hear myself trying to convince myself that it is time to get back on my feet and exercise the spiritual muscles that had not been used in the wilderness.

It could have been easy to wander in circles in my own little wilderness, even if I had managed to find God there. Eventually I wanted to cross over Jordan and find my promised land. So it's time to get up and go. Are you coming too?

*

What is prayer?

JAMES 4:1–17

So give yourselves humbly to God. Resist the devil and he will flee from you. And when you draw close to God, God will draw close to you. Wash your hands, you sinners, and let your hearts be filled with God alone to make them pure and true to him.

Many people over the centuries have written about prayer and its dynamics but, for me, prayer is simply drawing near to God in order that he can draw near to us. Finding ways to enter and stay in an awareness of God's presence is something I have covered earlier, as is humility, the attribute we need in order to desire to be in God's presence at all. Prayer is what happens when you are in God's presence: it is an umbrella term that covers a multitude of manners of communication.

There are many people in our church who are giants of prayer. It can be very easy to feel daunted by the commitment of people like that and to think that it's not worth trying at all because you haven't got the time or energy to devote to prayer in the same way that they do. You would be right to think that you might not be able to pray in the same way, but wrong to think that it's not worth starting at all. For the busy parent or carer, daily intercession meetings may not be on the agenda, but God is happy to be acknowledged in many other ways, more in keeping with your situation.

Sometimes you will only have enough time and energy, as you sit on the side of the bed in the morning, to sigh, breathing in the Spirit and whispering, 'I desire you, Lord, and to do your will. Strengthen me.' You can be sure that God draws near and honours your approach to him.

The purpose of prayer is to invite God to live inside us, so our greatest desire is always to obey his will. The mind thus becomes the temple of God, and the soul becomes his friend.

BASIL (c.330–379)

*

The Lord, my comfort

PSALM 119:75–91

Now let your lovingkindness comfort me, just as you promised. Surround me with your tender mercies, that I may live. For your law is my delight… Help me to love your every wish; then I will never have to be ashamed of myself. I faint for your salvation; but I expect your help, for you have promised it.

When we are busy and stressed, it can be a long time before we realize that we haven't stopped for more than an early morning sigh of prayer or really spent time with God. It is the same feeling you get when you realize that life has become so hectic that you and your loved one have not sat down and given each other a chance to have a really good talk. If you haven't spoken deeply for a while, it can be difficult to know where to begin. Often it's best simply to rest in each other's company, drawing reassurance from each other until the moment to talk arrives.

It can be the same with us and the Lord. He is always with us, but if we haven't really spoken to him for a while, we can think that God must be offended and won't want to hear from us. Actually, he is like the father of the prodigal son, waiting with arms open wide to embrace us as soon as we take any steps towards him. Then we receive what we so desperately need—to be wrapped in his reassuring embrace until we regain the confidence in our relationship to talk again.

Grab that 20 minutes when it presents itself, find a quiet place to sit, wrap a favourite blanket around you if you need an outward sign of your inward desire, and say, 'Here I am, Lord; enfold me.' Rest, and then eventually let the talking begin.

I saw that he is to us everything that is good and comfortable for us. He is our clothing which for love enwraps us, holds us, and all encloses us because of his tender love, so that he may never leave us.

JULIAN OF NORWICH[1]

＊

Letting it all out

PSALM 131

Lord, I am not proud and haughty. I don't think myself better than others. I don't pretend to 'know it all'. I am quiet now before the Lord, just as a child who is weaned from the breast. Yes, my begging has been stilled. O Israel, you too should quietly trust in the Lord—now, and always.

I was sent a card recently with this verse printed on it. The picture on the front was of a small baby asleep on its mother's shoulder. The baby may have been asleep, but it was not old enough to be weaned and was soon going to wake up and become angry and demanding again. It would be months before that baby would be old enough to sit on its mother's knee without rummaging!

In the previous reading, I suggested sitting quietly wrapped up in the Lord's love. Like the baby, however, we will be able to sit like that for only a certain length of time before we start allowing all the unresolved conflict inside us to rise up to the surface.

It is a valid form of prayer to let this flotsam wash up at the feet of God in a storm of emotion—the psalmists did it all the time. You have to be quite secure in the love of the person to whom you are speaking in order to 'let it all out' this way, but God loves us so much that I am sure he would rather have all the junk out than in. Once we have poured out our anguish and are ready to receive, the Lord can start pouring his comfort into those sore places. God is like the mother implicit in Psalm 131: one of the Old Testament names for God is El Shaddai, and one of the connotations of that name is 'the God who breast-feeds!' Once we have calmed down enough to receive, God will give us more than enough to satisfy.

Lord, I have a lot of catching up to do with you. Just let me pour it all out before you today, and then please satisfy me with your comfort. Amen

*

Out of the depths

PSALM 130

O Lord, from the depths of despair I cry for your help: 'Hear me! Answer! Help me!' Lord, if you keep in mind our sins then who can ever get an answer to his prayers? But you forgive! What an awesome thing this is! That is why I wait expectantly, trusting God to help, for he has promised.

A while ago, I was sent a cassette of these verses set to very haunting music filled with whale song.[2] At that time, my post-natal de-pression was over, but still not so far behind for me to have forgotten how sunk into the depths I had felt. The music reminded me of the sense of helplessness and drowning that I had often felt, but the accompanying words from Psalm 130 were an affirmation and reminder that my cries had been heard, that I had been healed and forgiven—because God had heard me.

We recently saw some large whales in a massive aquarium, and I was reminded then of this psalm and the music. The water was deep and dark, cold and expansive. I was so absorbed in the whales and the vastness of the aquarium, I didn't realize until too late that I was about to be soaked in freezing water, as the whales deliberately created a wave at the direction of their trainer. When it happened, it was quite a shock.

When we cry to God out of the depths, absorbed by the deep, dark expanse of the situation in which we find ourselves, we may not be able to see the larger picture—the whole of God's perspective—but he does answer us. Like the deluge of cold water I experienced at the aquarium, he can break through our self-absorption when we least expect it; waking us up and helping us to see the healing and forgiveness we need. Are you prepared for that?

Lord, there are times when I feel as if I am drowning—in tiredness, in frustration, in my aloneness. I want you to reach down and pull me up. Prepare me for the shock of standing in your light again. Thank you that you hear, heal and forgive. Amen

*

Rest and wait

PSALM 37:1–8

Be delighted with the Lord. Then he will give you all your heart's desires. Commit everything you do to the Lord. Trust him to help you do it and he will… Rest in the Lord; wait patiently for him to act… Don't fret and worry—it only leads to harm.

As a mother of young children, I really need to hear these verses. It can be hard to delight in anything when your eyes are held open with matchsticks and you haven't the energy to clear up faster than the mess is created. But if I take my eyes off the chaos around me, look up towards Jesus and focus on him, then I can find a few moments' delight—even if I am standing for a moment or two at the sink, looking out of the window at the wren hopping along the dry stone wall without a care in the world. God cares for little wrens, so God must care for me. Lord, help me to hop as carefree as that little bird through the demands of my day!

Stopping and delighting in the Lord gives us time to let the worries and cares come to the surface and be expressed in our minds. It's a good time to commit them to him, even if they are concerns like having to make a special trip to the shops to replace a cracked lunchbox or finding time to sew a costume for the school play. Every time I stop and list all my worries and commit them to the Lord, the time and energy to get them sorted out always appear to be miraculously provided.

I have tried the other route: anger, fretting and worry achieve nothing and are very destructive. It is much better to sit and hug your grumpy child, forget about the mess and spend those precious minutes sitting down and giving all your concerns to the one who can help us do minor miracles.

Sit and list your cares, big and small. Commit them to the Lord, on paper if you want, and trust him to help you.

*

Hide and seek

PSALM 32

You are my hiding place from every storm of life; you even keep me from getting into trouble! You surround me with songs of victory. I will

*instruct you (says the Lord) and guide you along the best pathway for
your life… Don't be like a senseless horse or mule that has to have a
bit in its mouth to keep it in line!*

Do you ever have those days when if anything can go wrong, then
it probably does? I don't mean a string of trivial mishaps, either! It's
surprising how often this sort of day begins on a wrong note and
results in us getting on the wrong side of people.

On days like that, there seems to be no point in struggling
on regardless: it's time for some 'hiding prayer'. This is not the
disciplined kind of prayer that Jesus recommends when he says,
'But when you pray, go away by yourself, all alone, and shut the
door behind you and pray to your Father secretly, and your Father,
who knows your secrets, will reward you' (Matthew 6:6). It's more
of an 'I've had enough, and I don't know where else to turn but you'
kind of prayer. I suppose it's a bit like the 'rest and wait' prayer of
the previous reading, but coming as a result of more extreme
circumstances.

There are times when I have to stop what I'm doing and hide in
the Lord, and other times when I'm able to hide in him in the midst
of what I have to do. While I'm hiding, I'm also seeking him for an
answer to the problem that's causing the trouble. When all is said
and done, it is usually a matter of dealing with pride (think of the
senseless mule!). If we're truly seeking, then the Lord will point out
that pride and give us the strength to come out of hiding and find
the opportunity and the words to put things right with anyone we
might have hurt.

*I call on you, O God, for you will answer me; give ear to me and
hear my prayer… hide me in the shadow of your wings… O Lord,
by your hand save me.*

PSALM 17:6, 8, 14

*

Lord, teach me to pray

LUKE 11:1–13

Once when Jesus had been out praying, one of his disciples came to him as he finished and said, 'Lord, teach us a prayer to recite just as John [the Baptist] taught one to his disciples.'

The previous six readings on prayer may have seemed a bit unusual, but they were intended as an exercise in clearing out some of the emotional baggage you may have been carrying that might have made some of the disciplines of prayer difficult to cope with.

I think it was Teresa of Avila who said, 'Prayer is like a love affair with God.' Any of you who have been deeply involved with someone will know that anger, depression and self-absorption will not do the relationship any good; quite the reverse, in fact. It's the same with us and God: if you're harbouring anger and bitterness or you feel sunk in the depths, a prayer relationship with God is not going to be easy.

Having made a start at de-junking (and these things always take time), we will eventually find ourselves in the position of the disciples, able to ask Jesus, 'Lord, teach me how to pray.'

The disciples were keen to have a prayer to recite. This is a good place to start learning to pray: it is like learning the ABC before you start to read and write. It is a basic framework that can act as a springboard for our own words once we have got the hang of it. The framework of the Lord's Prayer consists of six points:

- Worshipping God for who he is.
- Asking that God will have his way in our lives and the world.
- Asking for our practical needs to be met.
- Asking for forgiveness and forgiving others.
- Asking for his help in the difficulties of life.
- Acknowledging his power and lordship.

*Read the Lord's Prayer, thinking about each phrase. Write a
prayer in your own words based on this framework. Don't worry
what it sounds like—we all have to start somewhere!*

*

The secret place

MATTHEW 6:5–8

*But when you pray, go away by yourself, all alone, and shut the door
behind you and pray to your Father secretly, and your Father, who
knows your secrets, will reward you.*

I used to find it almost impossible to find time to be alone when
I had four young children, a husband, and five animals in the
house, plus the parish on the phone and the doorstep—so I learned
to 'pray on the hoof', which taught me many valuable lessons.
Although, as the children get older, I am forgetting about the
exhaustion of caring for new babies and toddlers—a time when
even the quiet space of a night feed left me too exhausted to do
more than fling my unspoken emotions towards heaven—I have
returned to the realization that it is good to give God our regular,
undivided attention, as well as our continuous attentiveness.

Time and privacy are the big issues. Recently, as I saw the age of
40 approaching, I decided to learn to speak a language and play the
flute. After a while, I realized that if I was willing to find time and
space for those activities, then I had no excuse not to find a time
and place to give God my undivided attention in prayer.

This thought took me back to my time at boarding school when
there was no privacy at all: at one point I was sharing a room with
ten other girls. I remember being determined to find somewhere
quiet there to read the Bible and pray. My favourite place became

the fire-escape steps in the laundry room, shielded from sight by a stack of laundry hampers. No one knew I was there but God. Sometimes someone would wander in and out of the room, but they never saw me. And the reward? What can be more precious than getting to know Jesus better?

Lord, in due time, challenge my heart and my schedule and priorities, so that I can determine to make time and find a secret place where I can give you my full attention every day. Amen

*

Distracted by many things

LUKE 10:38–42

She came to Jesus and said, 'Sir, doesn't it seem unfair to you that my sister just sits here while I do all the work? Tell her to come and help me.' But the Lord said to her, 'Martha, dear friend, you are so upset over all these details! There is really only one thing worth being concerned about. Mary has discovered it—and I won't take it away from her.'

I am a very organized and tidy person. I find it difficult to sit down and spend time on myself unless the house is shipshape. I have had to learn that in order to make time for things I want to do, I have to make a conscious effort to ignore all the other tasks that need doing, or remove those tasks altogether by simplifying my lifestyle and environment to the extent that it requires minimal maintenance.

This is what I have had to do to fit in my new interests, and it left me feeling very challenged: if I was willing to rearrange my life to accommodate these desires, I should be just as willing to rearrange things to accommodate time with God. Yesterday morning I decided to do just that. I asked the Lord to wake me up early. I reorganized the morning routine to allow myself half an hour for prayer and a quick devotional reading. I was amazed how straightforward it was and how much better I felt for it. All the many distractions of the day fell into place in such a way that I found I was running an hour ahead of schedule all day!

As Jesus said to Martha, there is really only one thing worth being concerned about. If we are concerned about spending time at the Lord's feet, the rest of our problems and needs will fall into their proper perspective.

Lord, forgive me for the times when I have not given you the attention you long for and deserve. Forgive me for allowing my perspectives to become distorted. Help me to reorder my life so that you have the prime place in my affections and other concerns fall into their proper place. Amen

*

Making every moment count

COLOSSIANS 3:12–17

Let the peace of heart which comes from Christ be always present in your hearts and lives, for this is your responsibility and privilege as members of his body. And always be thankful... And whatever you do or say, let it be as a representative of the Lord Jesus Christ, and come with him into the presence of God the Father to give him your thanks.

When we have set aside time to pray and spent that time praying, it is so very easy to pack God up in a little box and carry on regardless until the next time we stop and pray. A real challenge of prayer is to take the presence of God that we entered during our devotional time out into the rest of our day. Most of us lead very ordinary lives and are not in what might obviously be termed 'full-time ministry'. Even in life's mundane routines, however, we can turn each moment into a living, breathing prayer by doing everything as if we were doing it for Jesus.

In order to practise this, it can be helpful to start by slowing life right down. We are all so rushed that we often miss the presence of God in the ordinary world around us. Next, we need to allow the Holy Spirit to prompt our hearts while we are performing a particular ordinary task: when I am tying the children's shoes I think of Jesus washing the disciples' feet, for example. I pray for humility and use the opportunity of the physical contact to bless the children as they go out into the day. When I am vacuuming, I think of the parable of the woman who lost a coin and cleaned her house until she found it—and I pray for the lost, people who need to know Jesus in their lives. Think of some practical ways in which you can slow your life down and turn ordinary tasks into prayer.

> *Normal day, let me be aware of the treasure you are.*
> *Let me learn from you, love you, bless you before you depart.*
> *Let me not pass you by in quest of some rare and perfect*
> *tomorrow. Let me hold you while I may,*
> *for it may not always be so.*
>
> MARY JEAN LORN

It's OK to ask

PHILIPPIANS 4:4–20

Always be full of joy in the Lord; I say it again, rejoice! … Don't worry about anything; instead, pray about everything; tell God your needs and don't forget to thank him for his answers. If you do this you will experience God's peace, which is far more wonderful than the human mind can understand.

I spent a lot of my early life having to be self-sufficient, so I often feel guilty about asking God for anything. I also find it difficult because a lot of writing on prayer emphasizes the need to avoid coming to God with a mile-long shopping list! This is intended to help people realize that there are other dimensions to prayer besides asking, but it does not mean that we can't ask the Lord to provide our needs. He knows that there are things we need and he loves to provide them (Matthew 6:8).

I often find myself so weighed down by something we need that I rush into the Lord's presence and come straight out with it, and then feel guilty that I haven't spent any time in worship, thanksgiving or confession first. It's rather like my children rushing in from school, forgetting to say 'hello' and blurting out that they need this or that, or asking if they can go to such-and-such an event. Once they know the answer to the burdens on their hearts, they have time for other chat! It's rather like me and God this morning: I had to rush in with my concerns about how to pay for some extra items I'd bought without thinking. I was more worried about how to pay for them than bothered about registering the lesson I'd learnt by my mistake. Once that was off my chest, I was able to stop and say a proper 'hello'!

Lord, thank you that you are interested in the smallest needs and problems that we have, so we ought not to have any worries about asking you. I want to spend time telling you about everything that weighs me down; please provide what I need, and point out what is unnecessary. Amen

*

Living in fellowship with Christ

1 JOHN 1

If we say we are his friends, but go on living in spiritual darkness and sin, we are lying. But if we are living in the light of God's presence, just as Christ does, then we have wonderful fellowship and joy with each other, and the blood of Jesus his Son cleanses us from every sin… If we confess our sins to him, he can be depended on to forgive us and to cleanse us from every wrong.

There are times when we find ourselves not wanting to talk to the Lord in prayer—usually because we feel we have been wronged or that we have done something wrong ourselves. The longer the problem gets left, the worse it becomes, until we end up not knowing why we stopped talking, and being too embarrassed to put the situation right.

In the children's prayer of confession that we use at our church, we admit our sins so that we can be 'together with God without it feeling difficult'. If we want to progress in prayer, we have to keep the relationship open so that we can be with the Lord without it feeling difficult. There is no point in hiding anything from a God who already knows our innermost thoughts! To stay in fellowship with the Father, we need to live a life that cultivates personal confession as an attribute, if not a discipline.

Confession is not quite the same as saying 'sorry'. Confession is actually agreeing with the Lord that a particular thought, word or action is wrong. When we do this, repentance (a real 'sorry') comes a lot more easily. Sometimes we need someone else's help with confession. Then, if we later doubt that Christ has dealt with the issue, the person who has helped us can remind us that the matter is forgotten. Confession is central to maintaining a healthy prayer life. Neglect it at your risk!

Lord Jesus, I want to be able to be with you without it feeling difficult. I'm sorry for trying to hide things from you. Help me to confess more quickly when I am wrong. Amen

*

Praying with others

MATTHEW 18:18–20

Jesus said, 'I also tell you this—if two of you agree down here on earth concerning anything you ask for, my Father in heaven will do it for you. For where two or three gather together because they are mine, I will be there among them.'

After beginning the adventure in prayer alone, it is natural to want to get together with others to share the burden of a concern and the excitement of seeing God's answer. Jesus promises that when we meet together like this, our praying becomes more effective for God's kingdom. This sort of praying is called 'intercession' and basically means that we are committed together to 'stand in the gap' (Ezekiel 22:30) and seek the Lord concerning a particular situation.

This sort of prayer is the spiritual foundation of many churches and ministries, which, without this undergirding, would not be even half as effective for the Lord. Although intercession is a special ministry, the Lord chooses ordinary people like you and me to undertake it. If we are humble and willing to accept the challenge, over a period of time we will become like the prayer warriors that we so often admire from afar.

It may be difficult when we first join a group of praying people. I am extremely shy in such situations. However, we cannot hide behind our shyness or fear for ever. Sometimes the Holy Spirit lays such a burden upon our hearts to pray for a particular person or situation that we feel as if we are going to burn up if we don't speak out. What we need to remember is that the other people in the group are there to pray, and are not waiting to see if you are going to make a fool of yourself!

We can learn so much by praying with others. Committing ourselves to meet and pray regularly with a small group not only deepens and enriches our faith, but helps us to focus our attention away from ourselves, thus bringing our own needs and concerns into perspective.

*Ask the Lord who you could be praying with—
when, where and how often.*

*

Praying in the Spirit

ROMANS 8:15–30

His Holy Spirit that speaks to us deep in our hearts, and tells us that we really are God's children... By our faith, the Holy Spirit helps us with our daily problems and in our praying. For we don't even know what we should pray for, nor how to pray as we should; but the Holy Spirit prays for us with such feeling that it cannot be expressed in words. And the Father who knows all hearts knows, of course, what the Spirit is saying as he pleads for us in harmony with God's own will.

There is much more that I could say about prayer, but I would like to end this chapter with some thoughts on 'praying in the Spirit'. I must make it clear that praying in the Spirit is not the same as the use of a 'spirit guide' or astral projection; these things must be avoided at all costs (Leviticus 19:26b, 31).

When we give our lives to Christ, the Holy Spirit comes and lives within us (Romans 15:9), and this is the same Holy Spirit who 'speaks to us deep in our hearts, and tells us that we really are God's children'. The Holy Spirit helps us with our praying. When we don't know how to pray about a disturbing situation—such as a natural catastrophe or a terrible disaster—we can feel a deep sighing inside us. This is the Holy Spirit within us, aligning our desire to pray for the situation with God's desire and purpose. Of course we cannot know what God would ultimately want in such circumstances, but the Holy Spirit 'translates' what we are longing to say into words that God is longing to hear. Praying in the Spirit is like a long-play video cassette played at normal speed: we can't understand it, but God has the ability to understand it perfectly.

The wonderful thing about praying in the Spirit is that it is very easy to do anywhere—it hardly needs any thought, just the ability to slip into God's presence in the stillness of your heart.

Lord, let me slip into your presence in the quiet spaces you give me today and allow your Holy Spirit to pray through me. Amen

DONALD S. WHITNEY, *SPIRITUAL DISCIPLINES FOR THE CHRISTIAN LIFE*, SCRIPTURE PRESS, 1991.

---

1   From 'Revelations of the Divine Love', in *A Lesson of Love*, translated by Fr. John-Julian OJN (Darton, Longman & Todd, 1988), p.11.
2   Terry Oldfield, *De Profundis* (New World Music, 1997).

Ironing things out with God

Pray continually; give thanks in all circumstances, for this is God's will for you in Christ Jesus.
1 THESSALONIANS 5:17–18 (NIV)

Prayer is an unending adventure that is open to all our creative faculties. In the following article, I describe a uniquely creative way of finding communion with God in a job that I still absolutely hate. I think it must have struck a nerve, because it is the piece of my writing that people mention to me most often, even though it is more than eight years since it first appeared in print. I hope you find it useful too.

＊

It can be very difficult to maintain a devotional attitude in all the routine tasks that need doing every day. I have written previously about slowing down and consciously doing each task as if you were doing it for Jesus. It is very easy, however, to speed up again without noticing and then to realize that life has suddenly become rushed and mundane once more.

Keeping yourself in a place where God can touch and change you requires constant watchfulness and discipline, particularly in a chaotic domestic routine where space, quiet and solitude are rare.

I don't often have the house quiet and all to myself. One of those rare moments is late in the evening when the children are sleeping and my husband is not yet back from a meeting, but I know from experience that if I sit down for a quiet time then, I will probably fall asleep. Although mothers of young children need to grab sleep when they can, they also need to grab peace and solitude for reflection and prayer.

I decided to combine my rare moments of solitude and quiet with a mundane task that I really hate, in order to try to keep myself awake and use the time creatively to deepen my spiritual walk.

The domestic chore that I hate most is ironing, probably because there is so much of it with young children in the house. The tumble dryer broke down last month and is still away for repair, so the ironing pile has quadrupled, as I usually tumble-dry a lot of clothes to save ironing them. Anyway, this proved to be a blessing in disguise. Not only did it cut the electricity bill, but it gave me an even greater forum in which to develop this new spiritual exercise.

I started one night with three overflowing baskets of ironing. How could I possibly make this a spiritual exercise? I had read about a woman who had received the gift of tongues while singing worship songs during an ironing session, but that seemed a rather noisy option for my intention that evening, considering the lateness and quietness of the hour. I didn't want to listen to a worship or teaching cassette (I save those for cooking and washing up) so I decided to pray.

After a few items of clothing, I realized that I had drifted into brain-dead mode. I would have to try again. I suddenly had the inspiration to adopt the attitude of praying a blessing over every task performed. If I broke the whole task down into small tasks of ironing single items in succession, I could use them as springboards for prayer. For example, if I was ironing a school uniform shirt, I could pray for the child who owned it, and anything that pertained to their school life, not forgetting to give thanks as well as to ask.

To my astonishment, it worked! I now actually look forward to tackling the ironing pile in a peaceful moment and seeing who or what I end up praying about. Many of my prayers revolve around the family and the church, but as I get into the swing of things, I am able to use an item of clothing for thanks and praise, or just for wondering at the grace of God.

It would be good to demonstrate this with an example. Just as my husband Mark once had his quiet time in front of the whole church to teach by example about personal devotion, I will take you through my ironing pile into the presence of God.

As I get the ironing board out, plug in the iron and stagger into the kitchen with the laundry baskets, I pray that God will bless this time and use this task for his glory. I usually take off my shoes because it is more comfortable, and because it reminds me that I am on holy ground. (However, someone did tell me once that using electrical appliances barefoot can be dangerous, so now I wear flat shoes or slippers. Perhaps you should too.) By this time, the iron is steaming and I start.

John's stripy shirt: Thank you, Lord, that by your stripes we are healed...

Mark's clerical shirt that he wore when he preached last Sunday: Thank you, Lord, for what you are teaching us as a church. I pray that you would root everyone deep in your word, especially the new believers.

Philip's T-shirt with the crab motif: Thank you, Lord, for the unexpected cheque from the bishop's discretionary fund that will enable us to go on holiday this summer after all.

Tea towels: Lord, please bless the people who come to this house and drink our tea and coffee. Help me to serve them with grace, even if I feel interrupted and rebellious!

Philip's pyjamas: I pray for Philip, who sleeps very badly. Help him, Lord, not to strive for sleep, but I ask you to give him all he needs. I pray that you would help him occupy his mind with creative things while he lies awake. I pray too that you would help me plan time for him when the others are asleep and Mark is out.

John's pyjamas with Sonic the Hedgehog motif: Lord, I want to pray about the whole issue of computer games, trash TV and related issues... for my children, their schoolfriends and kids in general.

Hannah's pyjamas with the Lion King motif: Lord, look at all those 'circle of life' symbols on these pyjamas. Thank you that life with you is not a monotonous circle, but a straight road ahead. I pray for our children, that you would keep their feet on that road, and that you would remain close to them and keep them close to you as they grow up in this complicated world. I ask that, in all the mixed-up messages they get from today's society, you would teach them the truth and the truth would set them free.

My Sunday dress: *[Goodness me, did I really used to have one of those?]* Lord, thank you for this extravagant dress. As I iron the label 'Monsoon', Lord, I pray that you would continue to rain your blessings down on your people and that they would be so filled with your love that they want to bring others into your kingdom. Phew, this is a long hem. I thank you, Lord, for the woman who had the courage to reach out and touch the hem of your garment and was healed. I pray for all the women in our church who need your healing, especially................ And now the skirt bit. I pray for all the children that hang on to this skirt on Sunday mornings. I pray for our Sunday school leaders and I ask that you would deepen their understanding and experience of you so that they may teach these children to grow in a living faith.

Lord, there are quite a few articles of clothing in this basket that I can't pray out loud about here! I pray that if anyone reading this is inspired to use their laundry as a springboard for prayer, even these humble and private items might help them to pray about things they would otherwise find hard to vocalize... but, here are John's red pants, and I guess I can share that I'm thankful he is now potty-trained at last. Amen

I hope that gives you some idea of how I go about it. The whole process reminds me so much of Brother Lawrence, the barefoot monk who hated kitchen work but used it to bring himself into God's presence. This little quotation sums it all up very well:

We should apply ourselves continually, so that, without exception, all our actions become small occasions of fellowship with God... Since you are not unaware that God is present before you whatever you are doing... why not then pause from time to time at least from that which occupies you outwardly, to worship him inwardly, to praise him, petition him, to offer him your heart and thank him?[1]

Now what chore can I apply that to next? Sweeping the stairs, changing the beds, cleaning the bath... I wonder?

This is a revision of the article 'Ironing Things Out with God' which appeared in *Renewal* 234, November 1995, pages 28–29, and *Day by Day with God*, May–August 1998, pages 144–147. Used with permission.

1   Brother Lawrence, *The Practice of the Presence of God*, pp. 68, 69.

Guidance

The Lord will guide you always; he will satisfy your needs in a sun-scorched land and will strengthen your frame.
ISAIAH 58:11a (NIV)

These lines were part of a verse given to me by a woman who had 'waited on the Lord' for each wife of each ordinand who left theological college the year my husband was ordained deacon. She was very sorry that this was the verse that God had given her for me. She thought it was very negative: no one wants to go out thinking that the years to come are going to be a sun-scorched land. But she had heard right and, as you know, the following years were a wilderness for me. There are two promises here that the Lord kept faithfully, however: despite the emotional and spiritual hardships, he strengthened me enough to see me through and, eventually, satisfied my every need. The Lord is there guiding us even when we can't see him, providing for us even when the hand that gives seems to be invisible. In the dark days, don't forget that.

Slowly there came a point when I could see that the edge of the wilderness was within reach. I needed to know what the Lord had for me over the horizon, what I was to do and when. I had made so many presumptuous mistakes in my earlier life, by not really committing my way to the Lord and asking him to direct my paths, that this time I wanted to get it right. The following Bible readings were the result of my exploration of how we can tell if the guidance we are getting about the way ahead is really from the Lord.

*

God's plans

JEREMIAH 29:8–14

For I know the plans I have for you, says the Lord. They are plans for good and not for evil, to give you a future and a hope. In those days when you pray, I will listen. You will find me when you seek me, if you look for me in earnest.

When I was a young Christian, I was taught that God loves me and has a wonderful plan for my life. When we let Jesus into our heart, one change is that the randomness and aimlessness of life disappear. We grow to know and understand the deep love that God the Father has for us in Christ Jesus and that we have been chosen to belong to his family for a special reason. From then on, there is a new purposefulness to our lives.

Our primary purpose in loving God is to praise him and bring glory to his name (Ephesians 1:11–12). Praising God is relatively straightforward, but bringing glory to his name isn't just a matter of worshipping him on your own or in a church service. It involves seeking to do God's will at all times and in all circumstances.

As Christians trying to find out what living in the will of God means personally in a particular situation, especially if an important decision is to be made, we often talk about 'seeking God's guidance'. Seeking God's guidance about how he wants us to live for him is intimately bound up in many of the spiritual disciplines and attributes we have touched on so far in this book. If we are living in God's presence, listening to him moment by moment, submitting to him, praying, and loving others, then hearing the guiding voice of the Lord is much easier. That is one reason why I've placed this subject near the end of the book. The other reason is that, having read this far, you may find that God is changing you from the inside out and that you need to know his guidance for the new phase that lies ahead.

Thank you, Lord, that you do have a wonderful plan for my life.
Help me to know it and follow it. Amen

*

Listening to the right voices

GALATIANS 5:16–26

I advise you to obey only the Holy Spirit's instructions. He will tell you where to go and what to do, and then you won't always be doing the wrong things your evil nature wants you to. For we naturally love to do evil things that are just the opposite of the things that the Holy Spirit tells us to do… Let me tell you… that anyone living that kind of life will not inherit the kingdom of God.

Everyone needs direction and purpose and, as Christians, we know that our purpose is to serve the Lord and our direction is heaven-wards. Before we knew Christ, perhaps we found direction and purpose in things we now know God wouldn't want us to prioritize: many people are guided by the selfish human instincts that drive us to want more money and power and to gratify our physical needs. Other people realize that there is a spiritual dimension to life and look for meaning, guidance and direction in all sorts of spiritual practices that are not compatible with Christian belief.

As we approached the year 2000, there was an explosion of interest in what the future might hold and where the world was heading. People were not only looking to experts in economics, sociology, ecology and computer technology for the answers, but to people who claimed to have all kinds of mystical insights. The Bible makes it perfectly clear that God prefers those who follow him to depend on him for the future and to trust him for what remains unseen and unknown (Hebrews 11:1).

The Bible also makes it clear that we shouldn't seek guidance from worldly-minded 'prophets' and spiritualists (Jeremiah 29:8–9, NIV; Leviticus 19:31). This doesn't only mean that we must filter the opinions of the media experts through the word of God but that we shouldn't seek guidance through horoscopes, astral readings, tarot cards, clairvoyants and the like (Deuteronomy 18:9–11).

Lord, help me to listen to the voice of your Holy Spirit
and point out the basic human impulses and secular voices
you would rather I ignored. Amen

*

Acknowledging God

PROVERBS 3:1–15

Trust the Lord completely; don't ever trust yourself. In everything you do, put God first, and he will direct you and crown your efforts with success.

Another reading of this verse is, 'In all your ways acknowledge him, and he will direct your paths' (Proverbs 3:6, NIV footnote). If we want to know God's guidance and direction, we need to 'acknowledge' him in everything we do. This means putting every situation we find ourselves in, and every decision we have to make, into the framework of living for Jesus as our top priority. If we do this, I am convinced that the Lord shows us the way to go, what action to take, what to say or what to refrain from doing.

This passage encourages us not to depend on our own wisdom and understanding, but on the Lord's. He sees situations from an eternal perspective, whereas we see things from a limited human view. This can mean that we sometimes don't understand why God is asking us to do a certain thing. In those situations, we have to trust that he knows best (Isaiah 55:8–9). Later we are often given the privilege of seeing the result of our faithfulness, and this encourages our faith for the next time the Lord leads us to do something our human wisdom finds hard to comprehend (Acts 9:10–22).

How do we 'acknowledge' Jesus in a particular situation? I do it by simply submitting myself and the problem to Jesus in a prayer—out loud, in my heart or on paper—and then I wait for his direction. How do I know God's direction? It can come through reading the Bible, listening to preaching, the counsel of other Christians, listening prayer, the unusual 'coincidence' of circumstances, knowing the mind of Christ, the voice of the Holy Spirit in our hearts, prophetic words, visions, dreams and sometimes the audible voice of God himself! We will look at some of these methods in the next few readings.

Lord, teach me to acknowledge you in all my ways and help me to learn to recognize your directions. Amen

*

Knowing the mind of Christ

ROMANS 12:1–8 (NIV)

Do not conform any longer to the pattern of this world, but be transformed by the renewing of your mind. Then you will be able to test and approve what God's will is—his good, pleasing and perfect will.

When we become Christians, Jesus starts the process of changing us into the image of our Creator (Colossians 3:10). Jesus doesn't only come and live in our hearts and change our desires; he also transforms our minds, so that we start to become renewed in the way we think. We should never become arrogant enough to think that our walk with Jesus is so close that we know his thoughts with 100 per cent accuracy. Nevertheless, as the Holy Spirit works in our lives, we get to know more and more how the Father would look at a situation, what Jesus would do or say and what sort of things are in line with God's will (1 Corinthians 2:16; John 15:15).

We can nurture the 'mind of Christ' within us by making sure we feed our minds properly. This means avoiding mindless input (2 Timothy 2:16) and taking time to think about whatever builds our faith (Philippians 4:8). It is never a waste of time to review what you are reading, watching and listening to, and replace it with something more appropriate if necessary. The best food for nurturing the mind of Christ is the Bible. The more we read about God and his works, the better we get to know him and the 'mind of Christ' grows within us (Colossians 3:16).

Being fallen beings, however, we are so open to deception by the contrary voices of our human nature that it would be foolish to rely exclusively on our growing sense of the mind of Christ for guidance. This is why we need to sense what the mind of Christ in us is indicating, and then compare it with other avenues of God's guidance.

Lord, keep on renewing my mind by the power of your Spirit so that knowing your guidance becomes easier every day. Amen

*

Advice from God's word

2 TIMOTHY 3:10–17

Every Scripture was given to us by inspiration from God and is invaluable to teach us what is true and to make us realize what is wrong in our lives; it straightens us out and helps us do what is right. It is God's way of making us well-prepared at every point, fully equipped to do good to everyone.

The clearest way for us to hear what God is saying is to read his word, the Bible. Its teaching is as relevant for today's world as for the time when it was written. Much of its teaching is direct and we can find the answers to our dilemmas in its pages.

This is no use to us, however, unless we make a habit of reading the Bible and finding out what it has to say about various issues. We are encouraged to let the word of God 'dwell in us richly' (Colossians 3:16, NIV) and make us wise. That can only happen if we feed on it sufficiently. If God's word is in our hearts, the Holy Spirit will help us remember the things we need to know at the time we require them (John 14:26).

We must be careful, though, to read God's word thoughtfully, prayerfully and with reference to what it says in places other than the verses we are reading. We may also need to consider the historical setting of what has been written and decide whether or not our personal situation is comparable. Failing to do this, many people have mistakenly read the direct advice of scripture to mean one thing when it means something completely different. An example might be the woman who sought to divorce her difficult husband because she read that she was to 'get rid of the old man' (Ephesians 4:22, KJV), although the Bible clearly advises in many more places that divorce is not God's ideal for humanity!

Lord, teach me to read your word so that I might know your mind in a given situation. Help me to read thoughtfully and prayerfully, that I might keep my feet on the path you have chosen for me.
Amen

*

Learning by example

1 CORINTHIANS 10:1–14

All these things happened to them as examples—as object lessons to us—to warn us against doing the same things; they were written down so that we could read about them and learn from them in these last days as the world nears its end. So be careful. If you are thinking, 'Oh, I would never behave like that'—let this be a warning to you. For you too may fall into sin.

Not all the Bible is written as direct advice and teaching. It also contains many stories. The teachings of Jesus, and those of Paul and the other apostles, are often quite direct and are usually relatively easy to incorporate into our lifestyle. Yet we can also learn a lot about the human heart and God's desires for humankind in the stories of the Old Testament and the action of the New Testament, even though they were written in a different time and culture from our own.

By reading about the lives of people who sought to follow God, we can be inspired by their achievements and learn from their mistakes. It can often be enlightening to put ourselves in the place of a character and try to determine, honestly, what we would have done in their situation. In this way we can discover the weaknesses in our own character that God wants to address and the strengths that he can use for his kingdom.

We can also discover a lot about the nature of God in these stories—his holiness and righteousness, his anger and judgment, but also his compassion and mercy. Deepening our understanding about God helps to mould our own character into line with how he wants us to be and how he wants us to relate to him. This in turn affects the decisions we make and is a subtle way in which the Lord guides us, often without us realizing it.

Thank you, Lord, for the object lessons in your word. Help us to understand what you are trying to teach us through them, so that we can use those lessons to guide us through life. Amen

*

The word and the Spirit

1 CORINTHIANS 2:9–10

That is what is meant by the Scriptures which say that no mere man has ever seen, heard or even imagined what wonderful things God has ready for those who love the Lord. But we know about these things because God has sent his Spirit to tell us, and his Spirit searches out and shows us all of God's deepest secrets.

When we read the Bible prayerfully, sometimes a particular verse seems to jump out of the page at us. It's as if the Lord is speaking to us directly. This happens because the Bible is the inspired word of God, which means that it is 'living and active' (Hebrews 4:12, NIV). If we allow the Holy Spirit to illuminate our thinking when we read it, the words of scripture often have a penetrating and incisive relevance to our personal situation.

I am not talking about extracting chosen passages from the Bible and twisting them to fit our own needs, but learning how to recognize the voice of the Spirit when he wants to guide us using the word of God. When this happens, we feel our hearts burn within us, just like the disciples who walked and talked with the risen Jesus when he explained the scriptures to them on the way to Emmaus (Luke 24:25–32).

Let me give one personal example. In Revelation 3:8 (NIV) it reads, 'See, I have placed before you an open door that no one can shut.' I felt the Lord impress this verse on my heart very strongly just before my fourth child was born. I felt he was saying that new opportunities would open up for me and, because these opportunities were God-given, no one would be able to take them away from me. As it turned out, it took two or three years before I began to see what this might entail, but a promise of hope had been put in my heart and woken me up to possibilities that I might otherwise have passed by.

O Lord, speak personally to me through your word; open my eyes to see and my ears to hear. Amen

*

Listening for his voice

JOHN 10:1–13

Jesus said… 'The sheep hear his voice and come to him; and he calls his own sheep by name and leads them out. He walks ahead of them; and they follow him, for they recognize his voice. They won't follow a stranger but will run from him, for they don't recognize his voice.'

We don't hear the voice of God just through the written word, but also through the immediate revelation of the Holy Spirit. Because we have the Holy Spirit living inside us, we recognize God's voice when he calls to us (Isaiah 30:21), just as the sheep recognize their shepherd. We all have the potential to hear God in this way, but often we don't hear because we are not attentive to his Spirit. We don't stop and listen because our lives are busy and full of noise.

If we make time to lay our concerns before the Lord, and then wait for his revelation, more often than not he will bring a verse of scripture to mind that enlightens the situation. Sometimes our minds are drawn to see something in nature that helps us see the way through the maze confronting us. Other times the Lord will give us dreams, visions and pictures, but often we have to be content with knowing that he has the situation in hand and the answer will come later; all the Lord may want at that moment is the acknowledgment that we trust him completely with the issue at stake.

Sometimes the voice of God speaks into our hearts when we are not expecting it. After we moved house in 1992, I stood in the new garden and cried tears of joy to be out of the city centre. A voice in my head, almost audible, said, 'Don't get too settled; you won't be here long!' Although I didn't want to move again, I knew that the voice was the Lord's, and he was right—no sooner had I finished hanging the final piece of new wallpaper than the removal men had to be called!

Yes, Lord, I am listening… (1 Samuel 3:9).

✳

What about prophecy?

1 CORINTHIANS 14

Let love be your greatest aim; nevertheless, ask also for the special abilities the Holy Spirit gives, especially the ability to prophesy… But one who prophesies is helping others grow in the Lord, encouraging and comforting them… [and] helps the entire church grow in holiness and happiness… If you are all prophesying when [an unbeliever] comes in… his conscience will be judged by everything he hears. As he listens, the hidden things in his life will be laid bare and he will fall down on his knees and worship God, declaring that God is really there among you.

It would be very difficult to complete a series of readings on Christian guidance without mentioning prophecy. In secular circles, prophecy is understood as 'foretelling' and prediction. Though it might have some predictive elements, Christian prophecy is usually an inspired word of revelation. Some think that prophecy means 'preaching God's message from the pulpit', but Paul distinguished between the gifts of teaching and prophecy. Prophecy is a Spirit-inspired insight: it reveals the secrets of people's hearts and convicts unbelievers. For believers, it brings encouragement.

A prophetic word is the utterance of something that God suddenly impresses on our mind, often in a way that interrupts our train of thought, and always in a way that we sense is of divine origin. Such utterances, however, whether made in a public meeting or brought to a church leader for scrutiny at another time, are not to be considered as infallible. Prophecy is a fallible, congregational gift, containing revelation that is partial rather than complete (1 Corinthians 13:9), not having equal authority with scripture.

Prophetic words, when tested and found to be genuine, do have a contingent authority in the situation concerned. If they are a genuine revelation of the mind of Christ, then it would be unwise not to respond to them. We must remember, though, that it is not the 'prophet' who has authority, but the giver of the gift, the risen Lord.

Lord, you know that the thought of prophetic words may be a strange idea to some of us and that there is a lot to understand if we are not to be misled. Help us not to shy away from this gift, but show us how to use it wisely to comfort and encourage your people.
Amen

FURTHER READING

Mark Stibbe, *Know Your Spiritual Gifts*, ch. 6 (Marshall Pickering, 1997)

*

Test everything!

1 JOHN 4

Dearly loved friends, don't always believe everything you hear just because someone says it is a message from God: test it first to see if it really is. For there are many false teachers around, and the way to find out if their message is from the Holy Spirit is to ask: does it really agree that Jesus Christ, God's Son, actually became man with a human body? If so, then the message is from God.

Those of us who have come across a few wacky examples of Christian 'prophecy' may dismiss prophecy completely. Paul en-courages us not to scoff at the prophetic (1 Thessalonians 5:19–21), however, but to test it. Here are six tests that can help us.

Conviction: If a prophetic word is from God, there is a resonance in our hearts with the Holy Spirit within us. It leaves a sense of peace (1 Corinthians 14:33).

Community: The weighing of a prophetic word should be the responsibility of the community of faith, not just its leader (1 Corinthians 14:29). There should be an inner witness of the Spirit in the community as a whole.

Consistency: Is the 'word' consistent with the character of Jesus, the scriptures and the way God has worked in the past?

Christology: The Holy Spirit always reveals Jesus. Therefore, any prophetic word that does not draw people's hearts closer to Jesus should be treated with suspicion (1 John 4:2).

Character:	If the Holy Spirit has inspired the word, the character of the utterance will be one of love, not judgmentalism or elitism (1 Corinthians 13:2).
Consequence:	Jesus said of prophets, 'The way to identify... a person is by the kind of fruit produced' (Matthew 7:20). If a prophetic word is from the Spirit, it will strengthen the church, not tear it down. Checking this aspect of the word may require time.

Lord God, help us not to be blown here and there by every new thing (James 1:2–8), but to learn how to listen to your Spirit within us and to know enough about you, through your word and our personal experience, to know what is good and right and true. Amen

*

The light of circumstances

ROMANS 8:26–39

And we know that all that happens to us is working for our good if we love God and are fitting into his plans.

I have a friend, an elderly clergy widow, who is very keen on looking for 'signs along the way'. It is not as odd as it sounds. Those who have walked with Jesus for many years have learnt to recognize and assess the 'coincidences' that happen to them, in relation to the direction the Father would have them follow and the choices he would prefer them to make. If we believe that God has a wonderful plan for our life and that he knew about it before we were born (Psalm 139), then we are bound to see hints of that plan in what we experience, if we keep our eyes peeled.

Bad things do happen to good people, because we live in a fallen world that is currently not how God would like it to be. Yet, good or bad, the Lord is there in it with us. He may not be directly responsible for the bad, but you can be sure that the Lord is near to help us cope when our circumstances are difficult—and we can see signs of that if the eyes of our hearts are willing to look.

My grandmother always used to say, 'All things work together for good...' but she never finished the verse! When I became a Christian, I realized what blind dependence on fate that was, and that 'circumstances' will work for our good *if* we are seeking to put God first in our lives and are ready to do his will. Quite apart from that, 'our good' can mean something completely different to the believer than the non-believer.

I recently failed to get some funding that I'd applied for. I was so disappointed, but later I realized that the full-time study involved would have been an intolerable burden on me and my family. The Lord knew that, and fixed it so that I would have to study part-time. Thankfully I was awake enough to see beyond the initial rejection to what God might really want for my life.

Lord, open my eyes to see that what happens to me isn't as random as I think, and help me to see what you might be saying to me in it. Amen

*

Listening to leaders

HEBREWS 13:15–21

Obey your spiritual leaders and be willing to do what they say. For their work is to watch over your souls, and God will judge them on how well they do this. Give them reason to report joyfully about you to the Lord and not with sorrow, for then you will suffer for it too.

Over several years in the ministry, it seems to me that the last thing a lot of people do, when they are seeking to make the right decision at a crossroads in their life, is to ask their spiritual leader for his wisdom and prayerful advice on the matter. Very often the pastor is presented with a *fait accompli*. This often causes pastoral problems in those situations that go wrong, and the pastor ends up with the difficult job of trying to help sort out a problem after the event, when their help would have been more use beforehand.

People today are very individualistic, but it wouldn't do any of us any harm to involve other wiser, mature Christians, perhaps a home-group leader or prayer partner, when we are facing difficulty and have decisions to make. I know of some women who belong to 'accountability groups' and meet regularly to share, challenge and pray for each other. This is one way we can test what we think God might be saying to us, by throwing it into the open forum for prayerful consideration by others. The leadership of our church also operates in this way, so if anyone on the team feels that the Lord is challenging the church to move in a particular direction, the rest of the team can pray and discuss the matter to discern what is on God's heart.

None of us has a monopoly on hearing the voice of God accurately. If someone is dogmatically asserting that God wants them (or you!) to do something without due consideration, I would be very cautious indeed. To prevent disaster, we need to listen to each other, and especially to our leaders.

Lord, give me the courage and humility to be accountable to my spiritual leaders. Give all of us wisdom and ears that hear you, so that we can help those who may be accountable to us. Amen

*

Walking in obedience

HEBREWS 3:5–19

Today if you hear God's voice speaking to you, do not harden your hearts against him, as the people of Israel did when they rebelled against him in the desert.

Very often, we only hear what we want to hear. We close our ears to the bits we don't like and only listen to what's left. When we discern that God is speaking to us, we mustn't harden our hearts to what he is saying but should listen to it all. Listening does not involve only hearing, but also understanding and action. For the spiritual person, listening is the doorway to change, because they cannot hear the voice of God and remain unaffected by it. Listening to God should result in our obedience to him (James 1:22–25).

We shall be looking at obedience in more detail in the next series of Bible readings, but for now it is enough to say that if we hear the Lord speaking to us through the ways we have just looked at, the wise thing to do is to be obedient and act on what we have discerned.

A common theme running through my thoughts in this book has been finding God in the seeming desert of mothering young children. In the verse above, the writer is talking about the people of Israel, who heard God speaking to them in the desert, but hardened their hearts: they heard, but they wouldn't act. Hard hearts come from pride and bitterness. We've looked at the way humility and forgiveness work to counteract these ugly character-istics, so it should now be easy for you to see that a soft heart is needed to hear God properly. Only a soft heart will respond with obedience and turn God's voice into action.

The more you work to develop all these characteristics, which interact and depend on each other, the more your desert will begin to blossom and the hard things you have to face will become mysteriously easier to bear.

Lord God, when I hear you speaking in my desert place, help me not to harden my heart. I want a heart that yields, not one that rebels. Amen

*

Multiple choices!

DEUTERONOMY 30:7–20

Choose to love the Lord your God and to obey him and to cling to him, for he is your life and the length of your days.

Every moment we have to make choices. We have various options: (a) the wrong answer; (b) the 'looks-like-it's-right-but-it's-not' answer; (c) the 'almost-right' answer; and (d) the actual correct answer. Sometimes it can be difficult to know which is the right one! I hope that these Bible readings on guidance will have helped you learn how to spot the right answer in life's ordinary and unusual situations. Of course, the right answer is always God's answer. He wants to be our first choice throughout our whole life.

What happens if we choose the wrong answer? Deuteronomy 30:17–18 takes a bleak outlook on those who consciously choose the wrong answer, disobey God and aren't bothered about putting things right. I hope that the points we have covered in the previous readings will help you spot the 'looks-like-it's-right-but-it's-not' answer and avoid it. But what if we choose the 'almost-right' answer in good faith, and then realize we were wrong?

I believe that the Lord is compassionate as well as holy: he is the God of the second chance. We always get the opportunity to put matters right if we admit our mistakes and ask the Lord to help us sort out a situation in the best way possible. By some eternal mystery, even God's reserve plan for us is still his best plan: it must be, if he had our lives planned out before we were born, and knew what we would choose! That is part of the mystery of free will and God's sovereignty. We may have taken a bit of a detour, but we have learned more about life, ourselves and walking with God.

As we get to know Jesus better and how to listen to his voice, we will learn more and more how to make the right choice first time.

Search me, O God, and know my heart; test my thoughts. Point out anything you find in me that makes you sad, and lead me along the path of everlasting life. Amen (Psalm 139:23)

Perseverance and patience

And we rejoice in the hope of the glory of God. Not only so, but we also rejoice in our sufferings, because we know that suffering produces perseverance; perseverance, character; and character, hope. And hope does not disappoint us, because God has poured out his love into our hearts by the Holy Spirit, whom he has given us.
ROMANS 5:2b–5 (NIV)

The underlying theme in this book has been examining how to cope with an enclosed situation—in my case, mothering young children —when you feel that that situation has become a spiritual desert or wilderness. All along I've been keen to find God's positives in what could easily be seen as ongoing negative circumstances—because I believe that the kingdom of God operates an upside-down economy in which the poor are rich, the weak are strong, the last will be first and those that sow in tears will reap in joy.

Books are not often written in the consecutive order in which they are finally presented, and this one is no exception. The following article was the last part of this book to come into being, and as I sat and contemplated what I should write, I realized that no lengthy spiritual journey would be complete without some consideration of long-suffering and patience.

After the counselling session in which the Lord turned my life upside down and started me on the road to wholeness, I had no idea how long it would take to walk out of the wilderness where my bitterness, disappointment and depression had landed me. If we knew in advance how long something might take and the real measure of effort that we needed to put in to achieve it, there would be a significant possibility that we might remain sitting for ever on the starting line. Thankfully, we often seem to be shielded from the full implications of our initial teetering steps, and the Lord gives us the strength and vision we need for each part of the journey as we meet it. When we reach those natural spiritual vantage points where we see the next leg of the journey, there is time to rest and take on new provisions, to look back and look forward before we set out again. Life must be taken step by step.

*

Setting out into the unknown, even if it is a journey of successive legs, requires a commitment to persevere. There are no instant fixes and no short cuts, only the conscious will and self-discipline to keep putting one foot in front of the other, in the knowledge that we are gradually moving towards the future and the hope that the Lord has planned for us. Yet here is another tension: although we are called to press on towards the goal that lies ahead, we are also called to be aware and faithful to the present moment; this is what energizes us and keeps us going—the understanding that the future impinges on the present.

I have said elsewhere that 'now' is a gift—that is why it is called 'the present'—but it can often seem like a gift we could well do without. It may be fraught with difficulties and frustrations, trials and sufferings, especially if you are struggling to care for young children and struggling to accept the situation in which you find yourself. But herein is the mystery of the gospel: the willing and humble acceptance of our situation, the obedient commitment to stay and change rather than to run away and hide, submitting to Christ's 'easy' yoke, allowing him to help us shoulder our burdens and direct our steps, all lay down the long-term spiritual foundations in our lives on which Jesus can build more impressively in the future.

There is the need to be faithful in small things—the ordinary, unseen, undesirable tasks—so that the Lord can train and prepare us for the greater tasks that lie ahead. It was Mother Teresa who said that we cannot all do great things, but what we can do are small things with great love. We spend so much time straining for the great thing that God might have planned for us in the future—wishing away our present circumstances so that we can reach this goal faster, not realizing that the means to the great service, the great task and the ultimate honour is already in our hands, and is performed with perseverance, one small task at a time.

There is such power and energy released for good when the rebellious 'No' of our self meets and is changed by the unconditional 'Yes' of repentance and submission. The 'No' cries out from our deepest being, 'There must be more than this', but this 'No' is uncontrolled, destructive energy that will eventually destroy us. The unconditional 'Yes' to Jesus takes that energy, transforms it and moulds it to our good. Without the transformed 'No', the unconditional 'Yes' could easily become an oppressive, personality-quenching submission; but together they form within us spiritual character that can do the impossible for God. Look at Jesus in Gethsemane: the combination of his 'No' and 'Yes' produced the capability to endure the events that resulted in our salvation.

Washing 18 nappies a day, rarely getting more than 30 minutes' sleep at a stretch, and being stretched to breaking point by squabbling toddlers while I struggled to cope with the dark tunnel of my own wayward emotions, was no joke. It may not have been the same degree of suffering as experienced by Jesus in Gethsemane or the Christians to whom Peter was writing in his two letters, but it was very hard. Once my rebellious 'No' had said an unconditional 'Yes' to staying rather than running, to persevering rather than succumbing, there was the energy I needed to put one foot in front of another every day until I was through the wilderness.

We may not understand why certain difficulties happen to us. I still can't answer that question, but I do know that God is faithful—that 'when the train we are travelling on goes into a tunnel, we don't leap out into the darkness, but trust that the driver knows where he is taking us'.[1] I hate tunnels (I am very claustrophobic), but as a frequent visitor to Norway I've had to get used to them, to trust that the kilometres of darkness will end in the promise of light if I just hold on, look straight ahead, concentrate and keep going. Our spiritual life can be the same: we do meet times of darkness when we don't know how long or how far we have to travel until we are back in the light again, but we need to trust that the Lord knows where he is taking us, and to hold on to the end.

There are many who start out well but fail to finish because they don't have the strength and perseverance to see things through to the end. Jesus is not just the Lord of beginnings; he is the Lord of endings as well as of the journey in between. He not only wants us to start well, but to travel well and to end well, so we need to continue in our faith. That not only takes perseverance through difficulties, but patience—the ability to wait trustingly for what has been promised.

Patience is different from perseverance. If perseverance is the spiritual grit and determination that gets us through the hard times, patience is like the balm that tempers the overtly active nature of perseverance with the ability to remain resting quietly in God's presence. Patience is like the calm in the eye of the storm. Yet patience itself is active: it needs decision and determination to be exercised on our part, but like its cousins love, kindness and compassion, it has a quiet strength that spreads its influence like yeast in bread—quietly and slowly, so that we barely perceive it until it has achieved its task.

Patience also has the connotation of waiting, of hope for promised filling and release. You may be familiar with these words:

I waited patiently for the Lord; he turned to me and heard my cry. He lifted me out of the slimy pit… and gave me a firm place to stand. He put a new song in my mouth… Many will see and fear and put their trust in the Lord.
PSALM 40:1–3 (NIV)

If we are patient, the Lord will answer our cry. Until we receive the answer, we need to persevere. Jesus commands us to 'endure patiently' (Revelation 3:10), so we need to listen and respond, to be obedient to that step-by-step, day-by-day decision to accept what we have been given, but to strive for change.

Do not throw away this confident trust in the Lord, no matter what happens. Remember the great reward it brings you! Patient endurance is what you need now, so you will continue to do God's will. Then you will receive all that he has promised.

HEBREWS 10:35–36 (NLT)

---

1   An adaptation of a quote from Corrie ten Boom, a Dutch Christian who survived a Nazi concentration camp.

Trust and obey

Jesus replied, 'If anyone loves me, he will obey my teaching. My Father will love him, and we will come to him and make our home with him.'
JOHN 14:23 (NIV)

I can still hear the words ringing in my ears from my boarding-school Sunday afternoon Bible class: 'Trust and obey, for there's no other way to be happy in Jesus but to trust and obey'.[1] The beach mission chorus may give away my age, but the words are still absolutely true. We can never be truly happy in Jesus unless we are trusting him and obeying his teaching, or even testing and following the principles of guidance that we considered in the last set of Bible readings. There really is no point knowing what the Lord wants us to do unless we are willing to do it. As I mentioned earlier, real listening involves obedience. Listening is not passive but active: it should affect our choices, behaviour and actions.

Learning obedience also links in very well with our overall theme of living in God's presence. Look at the words of Jesus above: he promises that the whole fullness of the Godhead ('we') will come and dwell with the believer who obeys Jesus' teaching. If that isn't living in the fullness of God's presence, then I don't know what is. So my last section of Bible readings is on obedience, because it is only when we have learned that attribute that we can, as they say now, 'walk the talk'.

---

1 By Revd J.H. Sammis (1846–1919).

*

Command and consequence

GENESIS 1

When God began creating the heavens and the earth, the earth was at first a shapeless, chaotic mass, with the Spirit of God brooding over the dark vapours. Then God said, 'Let there be light.' And light appeared. And God was pleased with it, and divided the light from the darkness.

The next set of Bible readings will concentrate on the subject of obedience. I can hear you groan as you begin to dredge up in your mind all the thoughts associated with this word that imply obligation, duty and perhaps resentment, rebellion and lack of incentive. That is our fallen humanity rising to the surface in a knee-jerk reaction. Something we need to understand before we see how obedience affects us personally is the built-in existence of obedience within creation itself.

In the beginning of things, God created the world. When he spoke and said, 'Let there be...' the only possible outcome was that the thing commanded into being would come into being. There was no alternative: his word was and is the ultimate command.

We have lost our understanding of the magnitude of the power of God and his word. When we consider it, how can we puny individuals stand in the presence of the Almighty God, whose word can create a universe at a stroke, and say, 'I won't; I don't want to; why should I?' We have no inherent power or authority of our own and should not be surprised to discover that fact!

Almighty God, when I sit and contemplate who you really are and the power that exists in a single word of yours, I am amazed that my fallen nature dares not do or become anything that you ask, without hesitation or question. Change my being and my

understanding so that I instinctively know what you want of me and for me, and when it is you who is speaking. Help me to respond with trust and love rather than with doubt and hesitation.
Amen

*

Disobedience and mercy

ROMANS 5:11–21

Yes, Adam's sin brought punishment to all, but Christ's righteousness makes men right with God, so that they can live. Adam caused many to be sinners because he disobeyed God, and Christ caused many to be made acceptable because he obeyed.

If God had created us without free will, then obedience would not be an issue: like the universe when it was created, we would respond to his word without hesitation. But God did create us with free will: it was free will that allowed the serpent to tempt Adam and Eve successfully in the garden of Eden (Genesis 2:15—3:24). God had told them not to eat of the fruit of the tree of knowledge, but they disobeyed God and ate.

That act of disobedience spawned the myriad other acts of disobedience that have occurred throughout history, from the slightest demur to the most horrific acts of violence. Disobedience became an integral part of our being, our fallen human nature. Some people would say that this original act of disobedience not only affected and defined man's relationship with God, but also the balance of nature. They would contend that this is why creation itself does not remain within its preordained boundaries, and why disasters and disease occur.

In the verses above, we read that despite the disobedience of one

186

man, Adam, the obedience of Christ in his death on the cross allowed God to redefine our relationship with him. We now have the opportunity to put things right with God and live in obedience to him. Because Christ took our punishment for us, he gives us a fresh start if we are willing to make the decision to accept it. Obedience does not, however, become an automatic feature of our new life in Christ; it is something that we have to work at every moment of every day. Obedience is an ongoing, active choice born out of a new and loving relationship with the living God.

Meditate on the words, 'Your Kingdom come, your will be done on earth as it is in heaven.' Turn your thoughts into prayer.

*

Obedience and law

DEUTERONOMY 28:1–21

If you will only listen and obey the commandments of the Lord your God that I am giving you today, he will make you the head and not the tail, and you shall always have the upper hand. But each of these blessings depends on your not turning aside in any way from the laws I have given you; and you must never worship other gods.

At the very end of the previous Bible passage (if you read it in its entirety), we were told that God gave the Ten Commandments so that everyone could see the extent of their failure to obey God's laws (Romans 5:20). The Ten Commandments are the original ground rules of the old 'covenant' (which means 'promise'), which were supposed to help a disobedient people live in a way that pleased God. The passage above (Deuteronomy 28) shows us that obedi- ence brought blessing, and disobedience brought punishment and curse. The law of Moses was a very onerous system to live under; there was no mercy and no freedom to fail and try again!

Back in Romans 5:20–21 we discover that because of Jesus' sacrifice for our sins, we can now experience his abounding grace forgiving us, which is God's new covenant or promise. This doesn't mean that the Ten Commandments are no longer relevant. They are still God's ground rules and we must try, in his strength, to obey them. What the 'new promise' in Christ means is that if we fail, we do not need to experience curse and condemnation, but we can experience kindness and forgiveness—the Father heart of God (Romans 5:21).

> Take some time to look at the Ten Commandments (Exodus 20:1–21). Read them through and consider how difficult it is to live up to them and the ways in which we fail to obey God through them. If you need to pray for forgiveness, grace to change and the Holy Spirit's strength to persevere, do that now. Spend some time thanking God the Father that through Jesus we can experience mercy, forgiveness and freedom.

*

Obedience and love

JOHN 14:15–21

Jesus said, 'If you love me, obey me; and I will ask the Father and he will give you another Comforter, and he will never leave you... The one who obeys me is the one who loves me; and because he loves me, my Father will love him; and I will too, and I will reveal myself to him.'

For the person who has chosen to follow Christ, obedience springs out of love for the Saviour, not out of the fear of failure and punishment. Many people live under obedience more from necessity than love, and are often discontented and complaining. If we obey the call of Christ in our lives out of anything other than love for him, we put ourselves back under 'law' and do not live by grace.

Many people find it hard to obey God out of pure love because they have not fully understood that, in Christ, they are now adopted into God's family. As part of God's family, we do not have to behave like household slaves any more, but can live as beloved children. We no longer need to earn the Father's love; it is freely given to us through Jesus. There is no need to walk in obedience for any other reason than that we are living in a loving relationship with our heavenly Father.

It can be easy to slip back into 'doing what we know we should', because we start trying to earn the right to salvation again, or because God and other people are watching, or because 'it is expected'. When we let this happen, we 'sell our birthright' (Genesis 25:33) for something much less than second best . Every day we need to ask the Holy Spirit to keep our perspectives in line with God's. We are beloved children, not slaves, and our actions should be motivated as such.

Lord, give me a new and complete understanding of what it means to be loved as your child. May my obedience to you stem from this understanding of love rather than from any erroneous source.
Amen

Obedience and listening

JAMES 1:19–27

Don't ever forget that it is best to listen much… And remember, it is a message to obey, not just to listen to. So don't fool yourselves. For if a person just listens and doesn't obey, he is like a man looking at his face in a mirror. As soon as he walks away, he can't see himself any more or remember what he looks like. But if anyone keeps looking steadily into God's law for free men, he will not only remember it but he will do what it says, and God will greatly bless him in everything he does.

As we have already seen, obedience comes from the Latin verb *oboedire*, which shares its root with the word *audire*, 'to hear'. So 'to obey really means to hear and then act upon what we have heard; to see that listening achieves its aim'.[1] For the follower of Jesus, listening, hearing and obeying are intimately entwined and should all spring from humility and love for the Saviour.

When I talk to my children, it can be quite exasperating. I have to say what is needed three or four times, and even then my words may not get a response! There are three problems: first, I am not catching their attention before I speak; second, when I do speak, perhaps they are not expecting it because they are preoccupied in their own little world; and third, when I get their attention and they have heard me, they don't always do what is asked because they don't like it, don't want to or can't be bothered!

I know that we can be the same with our heavenly Father. First, we don't expect him to speak; then, when he does, we don't hear; and if God does get us to hear, we don't always want to obey. Time to grow up?

Lord, when you speak to me, don't let me ignore your voice like a fleeting reflection in a mirror, but let it be printed on my heart with indelible ink so that I am constantly reminded to act. Amen

*

Obedience and action

MATTHEW 21:28–32

Jesus said, 'A man with two sons told the older boy, "Son, go out and work on the farm today." "I won't," he answered, but later he changed his mind and went. Then the father told the youngest, "You go!" and he said, "Yes, sir, I will." But he didn't. Which of the two was obeying his father?' They replied, 'The first, of course.'

These two sons definitely heard what their father was asking them to do, but they both gave very different answers and then both did the opposite of what they had said. Jesus says that we are very blessed if we not only hear his words but obey them (Luke 11:28). It is not acceptable to say, 'Yes, Lord,' and then fail to turn consent into action.

When we find that our response to the Lord is like the younger son's, we must examine our hearts and ask the Lord to remove whatever is stopping us doing what we have said we will do. When our spirit is willing, but the flesh is weak, we need the discipline and strength of the Holy Spirit to help us do what is required of us. Occasionally this can mean rearranging our whole lifestyle so that our priorities permit and facilitate willing obedience. That is quite a challenge.

Most often, we are like the older son: we are honest enough to admit we don't want to do what is required but, after a little while, when we have had time for prayerful reconsideration, we do it anyway. In this situation we need to take care that our actions aren't totally motivated by guilt for not wanting to obey in the first instance, but more by our love for the Saviour and our remorse over our selfishness.

Lord, help me not only to be listening for your voice but to want to do your will from the moment of asking. If I am hesitant and unwilling, help me not to be so proud that I can't stop and think again, and respond with a repentant, loving heart. Amen

*

Obedience and submission

PHILIPPIANS 2:1–18

Your attitude should be the kind that was shown us by Jesus Christ, who, though he was God, did not demand and cling to his rights as God, but laid aside his mighty power and glory, taking the disguise of a slave and becoming like men. And he humbled himself even further, going so far as actually to die a criminal's death on a cross.

Doing what we know we should, rather than doing what we want, demands humility and submission from us. We were set the ultimate example by Jesus himself, who humbled himself to become a man, and 'became obedient to death' (NIV). Jesus knew what it was to be human: he faced the same struggles that we face. We see this especially in the garden of Gethsemane, where he struggled to reach a place of acceptance and could finally say, 'Your will be done.' He knew it would be a difficult and painful path that would cost him everything.

None of us, however, will ever know the depth and intensity of struggle that Jesus did, because none of us have so much to lose: we are mere humans, not God himself. But if the Son of God was willing to renounce his rights as God, who are we to think that we can demand to hold on to our 'rights'? He understands our struggle and is constantly beside us to strengthen and help us when decisions become difficult, but his love demands our humility, commands our submission and graciously waits for our obedient actions.

Humility is the understanding of who we are before God. Submission is the acknowledgment of that understanding, which then leaves us no alternative but to obey, to act, in response to the undeserved love of God that we have received in Jesus.

Can you think of any situation where you have had to, or might have to, submit yourself to God out of obedience to Christ?

Lord, give me the humility and wisdom to recognize when obedience to you demands that I must yield my opinions, and what I consider to be my rights, for the sake of your kingdom. Amen

*

Obedience and suffering

HEBREWS 5:7–14

Even though Jesus was God's Son, he had to learn from experience what it was like to obey, when obeying meant suffering. It was after he had proved himself perfect in this experience that Jesus became the giver of eternal salvation to all those who obey him.

If we desire to follow the example of Jesus, we must learn to obey his word and his will, but we may need to learn to suffer as a result of that obedience. It is easy to be obedient when it doesn't cost us much and we have to sacrifice little or nothing in the process. We can then easily become a little proud about what obedient followers of Christ we are! The test comes when obedience starts to hurt. Obedience can earn us the criticism of people we consider friends; it can cause misunderstandings at work or in our children's schools. It could cost us our job, our home, or our professional reputation.

In the Western world, we don't have much experience of obedience causing us agonizing physical suffering and death, or the loss of family members and the trauma that accompanies it, but many Christians have to face these challenges every single day. Is our relationship with Jesus such that we could endure such suffering for his sake?

My mind often turns to the massacre of 20 April 1999 at Columbine High School, Colorado, when one teenager was shot because she was sufficiently obedient to her love of Jesus to stand up and say 'Yes!' when the gun-wielding youth asked, 'Does anyone here believe in Jesus?' What would we have done in that situation? I would probably have been hiding with the rest of the class.

What is the hardest thing the Lord has ever asked you to do? Why was it so difficult? In retrospect, what would have made it easier to obey? Would you handle the situation differently if you faced it again?

'Let us ask God that he be pleased to give us the help of his grace for anything which our nature finds hardly possible.'

ST BENEDICT

*

Obedience and 'sacrifice'

1 SAMUEL 15

Samuel replied, 'Has the Lord as much pleasure in your burnt offerings and sacrifices as in your obedience? Obedience is far better than sacrifice. He is much more interested in your listening to him than in your offering the fat of rams to him. For rebellion is as bad as the sin of witchcraft, and stubbornness is as bad as worshipping idols.'

In the story that precedes the verses quoted above, God had told King Saul to destroy the whole Amalekite nation, its goods and its livestock. But Saul, afraid of his own people, allowed his men to keep anything that appealed to them and only destroy what was worthless. He tried to excuse what he had done by telling the prophet Samuel that the animals were intended as a sacrifice to the Lord. God was not convinced, and Saul was rejected as king of Israel.

We also try to cut corners with God to make life easier for ourselves, while trying to retain an excusable semblance of 'holiness'. We make outward 'sacrifices', but we are inwardly disobedient. When the Lord asks us to do something, we must do exactly what he says, not construct an interpretation of the situation that makes it look nicely religious while working to our advantage.

King Saul chose compromise and dishonesty, and whitewashed them with excuses and outward religious observances. As a result, he lost his kingdom and everything the Lord had planned for him, and set in motion a future chain of events that almost caused the death of his nation in exile. Haman, a descendant of the spared Amalekite king, was the man who, as vengeance for the acts of Saul, plotted to exterminate the Jews in the book of Esther.

If we compromise and sidestep like King Saul, we will lose the blessings that God has planned for us, and could, without realizing it, cause hindrances to the advance of the kingdom of God.

Lord God, you can see all the little compromises that I try to hide from you: to you, they are as plain as daylight. Forgive me, and help me put these things right and walk obediently. Amen

Obedience to church leadership

HEBREWS 13:15–21

Obey your spiritual leaders and be willing to do what they say. For their work is to watch over your souls, and God will judge them on how well they do this. Give them reason to report joyfully about you to the Lord and not with sorrow, for then you will suffer for it too.

At times we all struggle with obedience to one another and obedience to those who have a spiritual responsibility for us. Submission to others is not considered an important spiritual discipline these days. We are encouraged by secular thought to do what we want and not to be influenced by others. This can make the role of Christian leaders onerous. It is difficult to lead a group of people, each of whom thinks that God is calling the church in the direction that suits their opinions and who find it difficult to catch the vision of the church leadership. But part of our calling as followers of Christ is to learn to submit to each other in love, and that includes to *responsible leadership*. Initially we may have to force ourselves to accept something that we struggle with, but then our willing submission suddenly makes it a joy to collaborate with Christ.

Let me be clear, however, that blind obedience is not the same as submission. Critical facilities are neither wrong nor irrelevant, especially in an age where many have experienced spiritual abuse from those in leadership. Sometimes we need to be reassured that the leaders the Lord has placed over us are doing their utmost to discern the will of God on our behalf as individuals and a community. In these situations we must feel free to ask with the right attitude, rather than murmuring among ourselves and stirring up unsettling emotions in others. Any leadership worth its salt is ready to listen to the people they are leading.

Lord, help me to be ready to listen to those in spiritual authority over me. When I find their opinions difficult, help me to search my heart for the reasons why, and give me discernment, love and humility in any questions I have to bring. Amen

*

Obedience and parenthood

EPHESIANS 6:1–4

Children, obey your parents; this is the right thing to do because God has placed them in authority over you. Honour your father and mother. This is the first of God's Ten Commandments that ends with a promise. And this is the promise: that if you honour your father and mother, yours will be a long life, full of blessing.

And now a word to you parents. Don't keep scolding and nagging your children, making them angry and resentful. Rather, bring them up with the loving discipline the Lord himself approves, with suggestions and godly advice.

The issue of obedience within the family is a contentious one, especially if we have a parent or spouse who doesn't follow Jesus. The Bible is clear that children should learn to obey their parents. This lays the foundation for them to learn how to submit lovingly and willingly to God and those who will be in leadership over them when they are responsible for themselves and their own family.

We must be clear that our children's obedience can be expected and nurtured only if we bring them up in the loving discipline of the Lord, not making unreasonable demands or expecting them to do things that are beyond God's laws. There should also be room for all parties to learn to ask for and receive forgiveness when necessary.

Unlike our heavenly Father, we often make parenting mistakes! For the partner of a non-Christian spouse, and for those with unbelieving parents, it may be difficult to discern the line beyond which submission becomes unreasonable, and what sort of response to make in that situation. When disagreements become inevitable, we need to remember that respectful behaviour and a godly life speak louder than angry words (1 Peter 3:1–2).

> *Lord, teach us to be loving and respectful parents. Show us how caring for our children can break the cycle of selfishness in ourselves and in our marriage. May the obedience we teach them not be used for anyone else's selfish gain, but for the benefit of the whole family's growth in the love of God. Amen*

*

Obedience to secular authority

1 PETER 2:11–25

For the Lord's sake, obey every law of your government: those of the king as head of the state, and those of the king's officers, for he has sent them to punish all who do wrong, and to honour those who do right. It is God's will that your good lives should silence those who foolishly condemn the Gospel without knowing what it can do for them, having never experienced its power. You are free from the law, but that doesn't mean you are free to do wrong. Live as those who are free to do only God's will at all times.

The Bible tells us that there is no government anywhere that God has not permitted to be in power (Romans 13:1–7), so if we rebel against the laws of the land, we are rebelling against God. This can be difficult to understand if a country is ruled by an occupying power, especially when that power is used to abuse human rights, but that is not the issue under consideration here. In the time of Jesus, Israel was occupied by the Romans, but Jesus still said that the Jews should 'give to Caesar what is Caesar's' when he was challenged about whether tax should be paid to the Roman authorities (Matthew 22:21). We need to do what is right and pay what is due, so that the name of the Lord is not brought into disrepute.

Lord, help us to see beyond the boundaries of our own small concerns and understand that our system of government is in power only by your concession. When it is difficult to understand injustices in the system, help us discern if our indignation is a product of our selfish nature or an expression of your concern for people's well-being. Teach us to be as obedient as our conscience permits, laying ourselves open to your scrutiny and direction. Help us to be open to the possibility that you might want to use us as agents of change, whether by praying for those who have positions of secular power or as active participants in political life. Amen

*

When is it OK not to obey?

DANIEL 6 (NIV)

The administrators... tried to find grounds for charges against Daniel in his conduct of government affairs, but they were unable to do so. They could find no corruption in him... Finally these men said, 'We will never find any basis for charges against this man Daniel unless it has something to do with the law of his God.'

Unless we find ourselves living under a regime that is flagrantly breaching human rights for its own political end, the most usual situation in which we might find ourselves unable to obey those in authority is if we are asked to do something that is obviously wrong in relation to our walk with God.

Western society has become so multi-faith and politically correct that everyone and anything can be accommodated except the 'established Christian faith' that is perceived to have dominated the national belief and way of life for decades. This means that committed followers of Jesus can find it difficult to gain the understanding of secular authorities in relation to their beliefs. In the light of this 'open atmosphere', the lack of tolerance to the practising Christian seems totally illogical. Many Christians believe that this is a conspiracy by the powers of darkness to ostracize belief in Jesus at all levels of society without anyone noticing the changing tide. It is important that we resist this rising tide.

I withdrew one of our children from a nursery school because the staff could not understand why their project on Hallowe'en and supernatural darkness was inconsistent with our faith. They said they would have removed the witch's grotto and stopped the ghost stories for members of other faith groups—then why not for a Christian? As our society becomes increasingly inclusive, we will find more situations where it is difficult for us to comply. My example is small, but others struggle with Sunday employment, deliberate corporate mismanagement and other situations that would affect their family's livelihood if they spoke out (Matthew 10:17–23).

Lord Jesus, in the difficult situations that we face for your sake,
give us your Holy Spirit to think for us and speak through us, for
your name's sake. Amen

*

Obedience and reward

REVELATION 3:7–13

I know you well: you aren't strong, but you have tried to obey and have not denied my name. Therefore I have opened a door to you that no one can shut. Note this: I will force those supporting the causes of Satan while claiming to be mine... to fall at your feet and acknowledge that you are the ones I love. Because you have patiently obeyed me despite the persecution, therefore I will protect you... Hold tightly to the little strength you have—so that no one will take away your crown.

These verses speak with compassion and understanding about our human condition. We are not strong, but we try to obey even when it is a struggle to discover what God wants us to do and a further struggle to find the strength and determination to do it. Often we pay a great cost for our obedience and risk the possibility of persecution from others, including our own family. The reward, however, is that Jesus opens a door for us that no earthly or spiritual power can shut. We are welcomed into the Father-heart of God and his eternal kingdom, now and in eternity.

Despite the costs and the difficulties, Jesus encourages us to keep going in the strength of his Holy Spirit so that we don't lose our crown. Even when we do fail and wander away from what he had planned for us, God the Father is still standing at the open door, like the father in the parable waiting for his wandering child to return (Luke 15:20). All he demands is our humble obedience—the step-by-step submission of our will to the will of God driven by our love for Jesus, a daily choice to take up our cross and follow him so that we can eventually live in his presence for ever.

*I am always thinking of the Lord; and because he is so near,
I never need to stumble or to fall... You will not leave me...
You have let me experience the joys of life and the exquisite
pleasures of your own eternal presence.*

PSALM 16:8,10a, 11

---

1   Esther de Waal, *Seeking God*, p. 43.

The door of hope

Therefore I am now going to allure her; I will lead her into the desert and speak tenderly to her. There I will give her back her vineyards, and will make the Valley of Achor [sorrow, tears, trouble] a door of hope.
HOSEA 2:14–15 (NIV)

I began the introduction to this book with these verses and, as we near the end, I want to revisit them briefly. I have already shared with you how the years in which I suffered post-natal depression and the early stages of my recuperation were like years in the desert, but they were years when the Lord spoke tenderly to me and taught me so much about himself—and about myself. I have also shared how I had been promised, 'The Lord will guide you always; he will satisfy your needs in a sun-scorched land and will strengthen your frame' (Isaiah 58:11a, NIV), and how the Lord kept that promise despite the arid surroundings in which I found myself.

After years in the wilderness learning spiritual survival skills and how to find spiritual refreshment in the strangest of places, it would have been very easy to have grown so used to my surroundings that I decided to stay there: even adversity can become comfortable after a while. But God demands that we face up to the tension that exists between willing acceptance of our situation and the necessity of facing new horizons. He always wants to move us on to the next challenge. Spiritual growth demands change and we must be open and responsive to the path God prepares for us, even if it means being willing to relinquish what is actually a comfortable desert.[1]

As we seek him in the desert place where we think nothing will grow, the Lord allures us, woos us and deepens our relationship with him so that we become 'a well-watered garden, like a spring whose waters never fail' (Isaiah 58:11)—an oasis in the middle of the desert of our trying circumstances. In this fertile environment that was once desert, the Lord 'gives us back our vineyards', and what was once desert is desert no more. We look around in amazement, for the landscape has changed without our realizing it—because the Lord has changed us.

We may have spent years in the Valley of Achor but, almost without our noticing it, the Lord opens a door of hope for us there: 'I know the plans I have for you,' declares the Lord, 'plans to prosper you and not to harm you, plans to give you hope and a future' (Jeremiah 29:11, NIV). Open doors are an invitation for us to walk through them, and until we do, they remain simply doors of hope: only by walking through them, which takes courage, do we receive what is promised.

I cannot remember when I first noticed the open door of hope in my own desert valley of tears. In fact, there were probably a succession of doors that I chose to walk through, as well as a lot of shut doors that I tried to open in vain. What I want to emphasize is that walking through the offered door demands that we take the initiative: the Lord is not going to push us. To shift the metaphor once more: in the desert he may 'give us back our vineyards', but we are the ones who have to see them for what they are, accept the gift of those vineyards, till them, plant them, water them, weed them, train and tend the vines, and guard the developing fruit before we can harvest the fruit and celebrate (compare Proverbs 31:16–17). That can take several years of hard, steady work and lots of patience; it can even mean learning to cope with delay and disappointment.

This is the reason why I included a series of Bible readings in this book on recognizing the Lord's guidance. If we know how the Lord guides us, then we will recognize the open door and the unplanted vineyard when they appear and will prayerfully take the opportunities that the Lord offers us. Initially, the 'vineyard' may not look very promising, or the 'open door' may appear not to be leading anywhere very special, but the Lord is in the business of taking small things and turning them into something larger if we are acknowledging him in our decision-making.

When my children were still toddlers, I started to garden; they wanted to be outside and I had to find something to do while I watched them. Four years later, what had been a little vegetable patch was supplying ready-washed organic salads to the local greengrocer and a long list of private customers. I was eyeing up the field next door to the vicarage when (thankfully, perhaps) we were called to another parish. The Lord's 'alluring' obviously wasn't over; it had shifted emphasis. It was hard to let go of my 'vineyard' of a vegetable plot but, despite this, I knew the Lord had promised me that if I accepted the relocation and the changes he had in store for us, there would be better things to come.

As I shared earlier, the verses that were laid on my heart at a silent retreat a week before our fourth child was born and six months before we moved were: 'My lover spoke and said to me, "Arise, my darling, my beautiful one, and come with me. See! The winter is past; the rains are over and gone. Flowers appear on the earth; the season of singing has come"' (Song of Songs 2:11–12a, NIV). I felt like Cinderella being invited to the ball and, rather like her, I had no idea where the dress, the shoes or the coach were coming from— or, in my case, who would be babysitting child number four—but when the Lord allures you like that, you can't say 'No' even if you can't see what lies behind the open door.

I am going to surprise you now by saying that nothing happened for two years. We moved house and I had time to prove to myself that I could be a good mother. There was no depression this time— how wonderful—and I had time to reflect on all the lessons the Lord had taught me, by writing devotional Bible reading notes for *Day by Day with God*, and the occasional magazine article.

Then one day I found my babysitter (aged in her 80s) sitting on our sofa reading *Teach Yourself Serbo-Croat*. I sensed a door opening: if she could do something like that at her age, there was nothing stopping me doing something similar at 40. It took a while for this idea to percolate through my mind, but some months later Mark was going into town and I asked him to buy me a copy of *Teach Yourself Norwegian*. I sat and ploughed through it while I watched children's TV with our toddler. A year later I found myself in a language class with ten undergraduates at London University while our youngest was at playgroup. The next year I was back there again, studying for degree-level Norwegian and writing a dissertation on pre-modern Norwegian history while he was at nursery.

It seemed that the youngest wasn't at nursery long, and he would soon start school. I was considering doing a teacher's refresher course and going back to the classroom myself: that would fit in with being a mum and a vicar's wife, wouldn't it? This was a door that stayed shut even though I rattled it for a long time, and very hard. 'What do you really want to do?' asked my language teacher during the last lesson of the university teaching session. 'I want to stay on here,' I said, 'but I don't think they'll let me.' 'Ask,' she said. So I did. The door swung open, and I was accepted to study for an MA in Scandinavian translation—the only thing my new qualifications allowed me to do!

I accepted the offer and went forward in faith: I pulled out of the teacher retraining course and saved up all summer to try to pay for the university fees. Part-time study was all I could afford in time and money. On the first day of term I went to pay my fees with a cheque I knew would bounce, and went to the department to sign in. What a surprise was awaiting me: I was told that I had been awarded a scholarship and my fees were paid in full! To me this was the Lord confirming that I'd made the right decision and that the 'open door' had really been opened by him, however strange a door it may look to other people.

As I sit finishing this manuscript, I am rejoicing over the publication of my first translation,[2] waiting for the results of my MA exams and the projects that lie ahead. I would not say that life is always easy: mothering three teenagers and a seven-year-old is more than a challenge and I struggle along with the best of them, and my work is challenging and daunting as well as exciting. Yet the landscape has changed, the wilderness years are over and a new chapter has begun.

I share all this with you to encourage you that the Lord has something special in mind for you too—something that only you are equipped for—and that the challenges you are facing now are a preparation for what lies ahead. Keep your eyes open for your 'open door', your 'unplanted vineyard', but while you are looking, enjoy your time with your little ones, because time passes faster than you could ever realize.

I do pray that this book has been some encouragement to you. Let me end by sharing a short prayer that was left stuck behind a cupboard door of the kitchen I inherited from one of Corrie ten Boom's travelling companions 20 years ago. I pray it will bless you the way it has blessed me.

Lord, prepare me for what you are preparing for me. Amen

---

1 See my article 'Facing up to Change' on www.brf.org.uk
2 *Word Bytes: the Completely Manageable Bible in 365 Readings* by Knut Tveitereid (BRF, 2003).

Bibliography

A. Ashwin, *Patterns not Padlocks* (Eagle, 1992)

J.P. Caussade, *Self-abandonment to Divine Providence*, translated by A. Thorold (Burns, Oates & Washbourne Ltd, 1952)

W. Corswant, *A Dictionary of Life in Biblical Times*, translated by A. Heathcote (Hodder & Stoughton, 1960) (for insights into bare-footedness in biblical times)

E. de Waal, *Seeking God—the way of St Benedict* (Fount, 1984)

R. Foster, *Freedom of Simplicity* (Triangle/SPCK, 1981)

R. Foster, *A Celebration of Discipline* (Hodder & Stoughton 1982, 1989)

R. Foster and J.B. Smith (eds.), *Devotional Classics*, revised edition (Hodder & Stoughton, 1993)

R. Foster, *Money, Sex and Power* (Hodder & Stoughton, 1985)

S. Haydon-Knowell, *How to be a Better Leader's Wife* (Coastlands, 1983)

M. Hebblethwaite, *Finding God in All Things* (Fount, 1987)

Julian of Norwich, 'Revelations of the Divine Love', in *A Lesson of Love*, translated by Fr. John-Julian OJN (Darton, Longman & Todd, 1988)

J. Keiller, *Patterns of Prayer* (Daybreak, 1989)

Thomas à Kempis, *The Imitation of Christ*, translated by Leo Sherley-Price (Penguin, 1965)

Brother Lawrence, *The Practice of the Presence of God*, translated by E.K. Blaiklock (Hodder & Stoughton, 1981)

N. Page, *Keep it Simple: Creating Your Own Rule for Life* (HarperCollins, 1999)

G. Sherrer and L. Watson, *A House of Many Blessings: The Joy of Christian Hospitality* (Eagle, 1993)

M. Stibbe, *Know Your Spiritual Gifts* (Marshall Pickering, 1997)

R. Van de Weyer, *The Way of Holiness* (Fount, 1992)

P. Wilson, *The Little Book of Calm* (Penguin, 1999)

The Cloud of Unknowing, translated by H. Backhouse (ed.) (Hodder & Stoughton, 1985)

The Rule of St Benedict, translated by Abbot Parry OSB (Gracewing, 1990)

Why Men Don't Iron, Channel 4, Tuesday 30 June 1998